T0151289

Buffalo Bird Woman's Garden

Buffalo Bird Woman, 1910 (photographed by Gilbert Wilson; Minnesota Historical Society 9771-A)

Buffalo Bird Woman's Garden

Agriculture of the Hidatsa Indians

GILBERT L. WILSON

With a new introduction by
Jeffery R. Hanson

MINNESOTA HISTORICAL SOCIETY PRESS
ST. PAUL

Borealis Books are high-quality paperback reprints of books chosen by the Minnesota Historical Society Press for their importance as enduring historical sources and their valuable accounts of life in the Upper Midwest.

♾ The paper used in this publication meets the minimum requirements of the American National Standard for Information Sciences—Permanence for Printed Library materials, ANSI Z39.48-1984.

Minnesota Historical Society Press, St. Paul
www.mnhs.org/mhspress

Originally published as *Agriculture of the Hidatsa Indians: An Indian Interpretation*, copyright 1917 by the University of Minnesota

New material copyright 1987 by the Minnesota Historical Society
International Standard Book Number 0-87351-219-7

12

Library of Congress Cataloging-in-Publication Data

Wilson, Gilbert Livingstone, 1868–1930
Buffalo Bird Woman's garden.
Reprint. Originally published: Agriculture of the Hidatsa Indians.
Minneapolis. 1917.
1. Hidatsa Indians—Agriculture.
2. Indians of North America—Great Plains—Agriculture.
3. Waheenee, 1839?—   .
4. Goodbird, Edward.
I. Title.
E99.H6W74   1987   630'.978   87–20355
ISBN 0-87351-219-7

CONTENTS

PHOTOGRAPHS

INTRODUCTION

Buffalo Bird Woman, known in Hidatsa as Maxidiwiac, was born about 1839 in an earth lodge along the Knife River in present-day North Dakota. In 1845 her people moved upstream and built Like-a-fishhook village, which they shared with the Mandan and Arikara. There Buffalo Bird Woman grew up to become an expert gardener of the Hidatsa tribe. Using agricultural practices centuries old, she and the women of her family grew corn, beans, squash, and sunflowers in the fertile bottomlands of the Missouri River. In the mid-1880s, U.S. government policies forced the break up of Like-a-fishhook village and the dispersal of Indian families onto individual allotments on the Fort Berthold Reservation, but Hidatsa women continued to grow the vegetables that have provided Midwestern farmers some of their most important crops.

In *Buffalo Bird Woman's Garden*, first published in 1917 as *Agriculture of the Hidatsa Indians: An Indian Interpretation*, anthropologist Gilbert L. Wilson transcribed in meticulous detail the knowledge given by this consummate gardener. Following an annual round, Buffalo Bird Woman describes field care and preparation, planting, harvesting, processing, and storing of vegetables. In addition, she provides recipes for cooking traditional Hidatsa dishes and recounts songs and ceremonies that were essential to a good harvest. Her first-person narrative provides today's gardener with a guide to an agricultural method free from fertilizers, pesticides, and herbicides.

For many white Americans and Europeans, the very idea of farmer-Indians on the Great Plains is unfamiliar. Most people think of Plains Indians as the nomadic tribes who, mounted on horseback and free from agrarian ties to the soil, roamed the Plains in search of the buffalo. Hunters and warriors, provident with nature and fiercely resistant to subjugation, tribes like the Dakota, Comanche, Cheyenne, and Blackfeet have come to typify Plains Indian life. In "dime novels," fiction, movies, and history books, these Plains Indians have symbolized not only the drama and romanticism of the Old West, but a disappearing lifeway as well. The nomadic Plains tribes became, in the American mind, the quintessential Indians: standard-bearers of a bygone age, remembered for their noble qualities of courage, freedom, and a oneness with nature.[1]

The other kind of Plains Indian is one to whom popular sentiment and to a lesser extent historians have paid far too little attention. These are the Village Indians of the Great Plains, sedentary farming peoples whose ancient lifeways and contributions to history and civilization have gone largely unsung. In the Northern

[1] For a discussion of the Plains Indian as a symbol, see John C. Ewers, "The Emergence of the Plains Indian as the Symbol of the North American Indian," in Smithsonian Institution, *Annual Report,* 1964 (Washington, D.C.: GPO, 1965) 531–44. For perceptions of American Indians during the nineteenth century, see Roy Harvey Pearce, *Savagism and Civilization: A Study of the Indian and the American Mind* (Baltimore: Johns Hopkins Press, 1965).

Plains, the Hidatsa, Mandan, and Arikara (known now as the Three Affiliated Tribes) were once numerous, powerful, and independent tribes controlling practically the entire Missouri River Valley in what is now North and South Dakota. Their cultural adaptations represent a much more ancient and indigenous Plains Indian tradition than the "typical" cultures of the nomadic Plains tribes, which depended on horses introduced by Euro-Americans.

The Hidatsa inherited a cultural legacy that had long withstood the test of time. Archaeologists have named their lifeway the Plains Village Tradition and traced it back to A.D. 1100 in the Knife River-Heart River region of the Missouri Valley, the historic homeland of the Hidatsa and Mandan.[2] The Plains Village lifeway reflects a stable cultural adaptation to specific ecological conditions in the Northern Plains. Agricultural peoples built permanent earthlodge villages where they would not be flooded, on the terraces of the Missouri and its tributaries. From these central communities the people took advantage of the opportunities that nature provided. The river channel provided abundant fish, musselshells, and migratory waterfowl. The floodplains and bottomlands were used for garden plots and supplied extensive quantities of timber for building materials and fuel. The valley, with its characteristic gallery forests, offered habitat for a wide range of large and small mammals and birds which were hunted by Plains Village peoples. Finally, the upland prairie teemed with bison, which were the major focus of Plains Village hunting parties. Thus the Plains villagers developed a successful and complementary dual economy based on agriculture and hunting which persisted well into historic times (that is, after the arrival of Europeans).[3]

Agriculture provided the distinctive flavor of this lifeway. The commitment to permanent villages, the unique and complex architectural achievements shown in the earthlodges, the settlements and community plans of villages (see Figure A), and the ceramic traditions, all testify to an agricultural legacy that lasted over seven centuries in the Northern Plains. This legacy is imbedded not only in the soil but also in the lives, minds, and hearts of those who inherited it, nourished it, and preserved it. It is to these people, the Hidatsa, Mandan, and Arikara, that historians and anthropologists have turned for this knowledge.

Before the 1830s, members of a large and powerful Hidatsa tribe farmed, hunted, and traded from their traditional villages near the mouth of the Knife River. The Hidatsa were divided into three closely related subgroups who, from about 1787 until 1834–45, maintained distinct and independent villages: the *Hidatsa-proper,* who inhabited Big Hidatsa village on the north bank of the Knife River (see Figure B); the *Awatixa,* who lived about a mile downstream from the Hidatsa-proper in Sakakawea village; and the *Awaxawi,* who lived in Amahami village

---

[2] Donald J. Lehmer, *Introduction to Middle Missouri Archeology,* National Park Service Anthropological Papers 1 (Washington, D.C.: Department of the Interior, 1971), 33.
[3] On the ecological conditions of Plains Village people, see Jeffery R. Hanson, "The Hidatsa Natural Environment," in Carolyn Gilman and Mary Jane Schneider, *The Way to Independence: Memories of a Hidatsa Indian Family* (St. Paul: Minnesota Historical Society Press, 1987), 333–39.

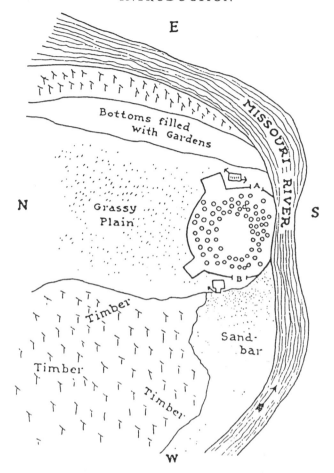

Figure A. The site of Like-a-fishhook village (Old Fort Berthold), which followed a typical Plains village settlement pattern (drawn by Frederick Wilson and published in "The Hidatsa Earthlodge," *Anthropological Papers of the American Museum of Natural History* 33[1934]: 341)

about one mile south of Sakakawea at the mouth of the Knife River.[4]

These subgroups had much in common. They shared a language, a family organization in the form of matrilineal clans (where descent, property, and subgroup identity was traced through the mother's family), fraternal and sororal organizations graded by age, and a cultural commitment to agriculture. The subgroups, however, had different origin stories, dialects, and ceremonial patterns, and it has

[4] On the subgroups, here and below, see Alfred W. Bowers, *Hidatsa Social and Ceremonial Organization*, Bureau of American Ethnology Bulletin 194 (Washington, D.C.: Smithsonian Institution, 1965), 2, 10–35, 64, 174.

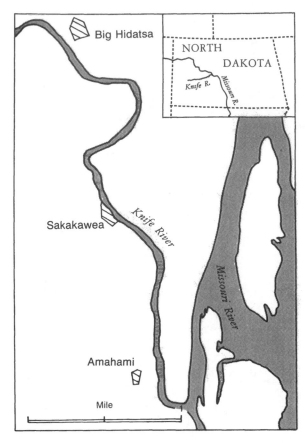

Figure B. The three historically documented Hidatsa village sites. Buffalo Bird Woman said that she was born at Sakakawea around 1839.

been said that they had no collective name for all three village groups before the arrival of the whites.

The events of the historic period bound the groups in an ever-tightening web of cooperation, unity, and interdependence. Battered by the smallpox epidemic of 1780 and increasing attacks by the Dakota, the loosely affiliated Hidatsa village groups created a tribal council around 1797–98. This council, made up of influential men from all three groups, sought to unify the Hidatsa in external matters of warfare, trade, and negotiation.[5]

In the early 1800s the villages of the Hidatsa and their neighbors, the Mandan and Arikara, became the focus for the Upper Missouri fur trade. Nomadic tribes bartered horses and hides for the valuable agricultural produce of the Hidatsa. During this period firearms had become a highly desirable item, and the Hidatsa regularly traded guns, brought by Canadian and American fur traders, to other tribes. The traders, who also valued highly Hidatsa corn and other garden produce, ex-

[5] Bowers, *Hidatsa Social and Ceremonial Organization,* 27, 29.

changed an array of other goods reflecting Euro-American technology, including knives, kettles, axes, and metal arrowheads. One of the most significant items received by Hidatsa women was the iron hoe, a tool superior to the traditional bison scapula hoe and one which greatly increased the efficiency of garden work. Bone hoes quickly fell into disuse.[6]

While the Hidatsa's economy was benefiting from the new commerce, their sedentary Plains Village lifeway made them increasingly vulnerable to enemies, both visible and invisible. In 1834 two of the three Hidatsa villages, Amahami and Sakakawea, were burned by the Dakota.[7] The surviving inhabitants of both villages sought and received sanctuary from the Hidatsa-proper and the nearby Mandan. It does not appear that either of these villages was inhabited again on a permanent basis. In 1837 smallpox wiped out half of the tribe, reducing the Hidatsa from approximately twenty-five hundred to about eight hundred. Survivors of this epidemic reorganized themselves at Big Hidatsa. From this point on, the destinies of the Hidatsa-proper, Awatixa, and Awaxawi became irrevocably fused. Reduced in numbers, beleaguered by the Dakota, and facing timber exhaustion, the Hidatsa abandoned their last remaining Knife River village in 1845 and established a new village, Like-a-fishhook, thirty miles upstream on the Missouri.[8]

In the shadow of Like-a-fishhook village was the trading post of Fort Berthold, built in 1845 by Pierre Chouteau, Jr., and Company (sometimes misleadingly called the American Fur Company) in an effort to reaffirm its trading interests in the Upper Missouri.[9] At Like-a-fishhook, the Hidatsa began experiencing the changes that would radically disrupt and alter their culture. Throughout the 1850s, 1860s, and 1870s, the Hidatsa (who had since been joined at Like-a-fishhook by the Mandan and Arikara) clung tenaciously to their culture and traditions. Suffering continued episodes of warfare and disease, the Hidatsa-proper, Awatixa, and Awaxawi peoples relied heavily on one another—and borrowed from the Mandan—to fill voids in their social and ceremonial lives. Changes beyond their control, however, were moving them in another direction. The buffalo disappeared from Hidatsa hunting territory; the presence and influence of whites became constant with the ever-increasing steamboat traffic and the military garrison at Fort Berthold, built in 1864 next to Like-a-fishhook village; the U.S. government imposed treaties that continually carved away their territory. All began to sever the Hidatsa from their traditional culture. The creation of the Fort Berthold Indian Reservation in 1870 and an assimilationist federal Indian policy forcibly altered the economic,

---

[6] The Hidatsa made a number of adjustments in their culture to the fur trade. For a look at these and other changes in Hidatsa culture prior to the reservation era, see Jeffery R. Hanson, *Hidatsa Culture Change, 1780–1845: A Cultural Ecological Approach* (Lincoln: J & L Reprint Company, 1987).

[7] Frank H. Stewart, "Mandan and Hidatsa Villages in the Eighteenth and Nineteenth Centuries," *Plains Anthropologist* (1974), 287–301.

[8] Hanson, *Hidatsa Culture Change*, 111–12.

[9] G. Hubert Smith, "Like-a-Fishhook Village and Fort Berthold, Garrison Reservoir, North Dakota," National Park Service Anthropological Papers 2 (Washington, D.C.: U.S. Department of the Interior, 1972), 4.

political, and religious structures of traditional Hidatsa, Mandan, and Arikara cultures.[10]

White policy makers worked vigorously to break up tribal patterns of the Hidatsa and other Indian peoples during the last quarter of the nineteenth century and into the twentieth. Indian reformers (almost all of whom were *not* Indian), missionaries, and planners of Indian policy generally agreed that assimilation could not succeed unless Indians were weaned from their traditional notions of tribal or communal landholdings and forced to accept the concept of private property and the values of the agrarian ideal.[11] Thus economic reorganization, religious conversion to Christianity, and educational indoctrination constituted a comprehensive attack on traditional Hidatsa culture. The breakup of Like-a-fishhook village came in 1885 as Hidatsa, Mandan, and Arikara families spread out on allotments along the Missouri River, tending to settle according to traditional tribal affiliation.[12] By 1888 the village was virtually abandoned—but the knowledge and memories of Hidatsa tradition were not. Despite the pressures of assimilation, and the cultural and psychological ambivalence that accompanied it, traditional ways held a firm place in the minds, hearts, and souls of many Hidatsa families who sought to balance the new ways with the old, to make sure that the children remembered who they were and where they came from, so they could accommodate change and not be swallowed by it. Ironically enough, it was one of these Hidatsa families, with traditional roots yet affected by change, that in 1906 joined with a remarkable white man in an ethnographic enterprise that not only broke through the barrier of assimilationist cultural repression of tribal life, but did so to a large extent from an Indian point of view.[13]

When Gilbert L. Wilson, an ordained Presbyterian minister with an anthropological and humanistic interest in Indian people, visited the Fort Berthold Reservation in 1906, he was introduced to Buffalo Bird Woman, her brother Wolf Chief, and her son Edward Goodbird.[14] He describes their relationship in his introduction

---

[10] On life at Like-a-fishhook, see Gilman and Schneider, "The Way to Independence," in *The Way to Independence*, 8–26, 128–58.

[11] For details of reservation policy as it affected the Three Affiliated Tribes, see Roy W. Meyer, *The Village Indians of the Upper Missouri: The Mandans, Hidatsas, and Arikaras* (Lincoln: University of Nebraska Press, 1977). For broader historical underpinnings of assimilationist trends in federal Indian policy, see Floyd A. O'Neil, "The Indian New Deal: An Overview," in *Indian Self-Rule: Fifty Years under the Indian Reorganization Act,* ed. Kenneth R. Philp (Salt Lake City: Howe Brothers, 1985), 30–46. For an excellent picture of the mindset of Indian reformers of the late nineteenth century, see Francis Paul Prucha, *Americanizing the American Indians: Writings by the "Friends of the Indian,"* *1880–1900* (Lincoln: University of Nebraska Press, 1978).

[12] Meyer, *Village Indians,* 135.

[13] For a description of Hidatsa cultural continuity, see Gilman and Schneider, *The Way to Independence.*

[14] On the work of Gilbert L. Wilson, here and below, see Gilman and Schneider, *The Way to Independence,* especially the essay by Alan R. Woolworth, "Contributions of the Wilsons to the Study of the Hidatsa"; Mary Jane Schneider, "Introduction," in Edward Goodbird, *Goodbird the Indian: His Story* (St. Paul: Minnesota Historical Society Press, Borealis Books, 1985; first published New York: Fleming H. Revel, 1914), xi.

to this book. Their long professional and personal relationship resulted in some of the most detailed (and for its time innovative) ethnographic material ever gathered on a single Plains Village tribe. In addition, Buffalo Bird Woman adopted Wilson into the Prairie Chicken clan and the Hidatsa tribe; Wilson became family. Interested in traditional Hidatsa culture during the Like-a-fishhook years (1845–86), Wilson relied on Buffalo Bird Woman and Wolf Chief as his prime informants, while Goodbird capably filled the role of interpreter and translator. From 1906 to 1918, Gilbert Wilson, often aided by his brother Frederick, an artist, amassed volumes of primary ethnographic materials bearing on aspects of traditional Hidatsa subsistence, technology, social organization, religion, mythology, and folklore. Wilson's highly successful formula involved two fundamental expressions: his own anthropological vision and the cross-generational changes in the cultural experiences of Buffalo Bird Woman, Wolf Chief, and Edward Goodbird.

Wilson's personal vision of anthropology cannot be understood outside the context of the intellectual philosophies of his times, both within and outside the field of anthropology itself. Anthropology in the United States was undergoing extraordinary change at the start of the twentieth century. During the latter decades of the nineteenth century, scholars had generally accepted grand, simplistic, and often racist evolutionary generalizations about the intellectual and moral superiority

Buffalo Bird Woman making a model corn stage as Frederick Wilson looks on, 1912 (photographed by Gilbert Wilson; Minnesota Historical Society 9447-A)

of "civilized" society over "savagery." This theoretical viewpoint was expressed by individuals such as Lewis Henry Morgan and institutionalized by the early work of the Bureau of American Ethnology.[15] Their approach—the idea of the natural law of progress from savagery to civilization, the unshackling of the human intellect from the darkness of tribal custom to the light of civilized reason—formed the ideological foundations for assimilationist policies such as the General Allotment Act of 1887 (also known as the Dawes Act). These "self-evident" truths, however, came under intense attack at the turn of the century, particularly under the influence of anthropologist Franz Boas, considered by many as the founder of modern anthropology.

Boas's fundamental criticisms of the evolutionary anthropology of his time concerned method and temperament. In method, Boas advocated a holistic, detailed, and exhaustive ethnography of specific tribes. In temperament, he was a proponent of cultural relativism, a nonjudgmental and empathetic attitude that recognized the fundamental value and integrity of all cultures, primitive or civilized. Thus Boas sought an anthropology with both scientific rigor and humanism, which were lacking in much of the evolutionary theory of the period. Boas taught these approaches to his students at Columbia University (among them Clark Wissler and Robert H. Lowie, both of whom knew Wilson professionally) and helped change the philosophy of academic anthropology. Outside academia, ethnographers such as James Mooney, Alice Fletcher, and F. H. Cushing of the Bureau of American Ethnology were paralleling Boas's approach in their ethnographic work on Indian tribes.[16]

Thus, when Wilson arrived at the Fort Berthold Reservation in 1906, cultural relativism and a deep appreciation for Indian customs and traditions were emerging as a counterpoint to the Victorian notion of the inferiority of tribal cultures. At first, Wilson simply planned to write books about Indians for children. Knowing that most such books were written and interpreted by whites, he wanted to tell about Indian life from the Indian point of view. When he became interested in studying anthropology, he embraced both the rigorous fieldwork and the humanism necessary to conduct insightful and productive ethnography. In 1908 he began collecting objects and information for the American Museum of Natural History in New York. In this work, too, the personal experiences of his Hidatsa consultants formed the basis for his ethnography. As he explained to Clark Wissler, the Museum's curator of anthropology and Wilson's supervisor, "We have abundance of material upon Indian culture, from white men; but telling us merely what white men think of the subjects treated. It is of no importance that an Indian's war costume

---

[15] Lewis Henry Morgan, *Ancient Society, or Researches in the Lines of Progress from Savagery through Barbarism to Civilization* (New York: World Publishing, 1877). A good summary of the evolutionary perspective of John Wesley Powell, founder of the Bureau of American Ethnology, is provided by L. G. Moses, *The Indian Man: A Biography of James Mooney* (Urbana: University of Illinois Press, 1984), 29–31.

[16] Moses, *The Indian Man*, 42, 224. A series of Boas's essays are presented in *Race, Language, and Culture* (New York: Macmillan, 1948).

struck the Puritan as the Devil's scheme to frighten the heart out of the Lord's an-
nointed. What we want to know is *why the Indian donned the costume, and his
reasons for doing it"*[17] (emphasis added).

Wilson sought to bring topical ethnography down to the individual level in
terms of personal experiences. For example, to study agriculture, he explained, "I
take Maxidiwiac (Buffalo Bird Woman) as the typical informant. I take her account
of a single year's work, in the main, when she was about 18 years of age. I follow
the seasons with her, getting her always to add all she can or will of personal experiences. Then I follow by getting all I can of Wolf Chief, her brother. . . . Obvi-
ously, a man and a woman are not going to look at things the same way. And their
differences, like the ms. mistakes of copyists in the New Testament, do not confuse,
but give us material to strike the true interpretation."[18]

The fundamental integrity of Wilson's approach is evident in his classic publications by the American Museum of Natural History: *The Horse and Dog in Hidatsa
Culture* (1924), *Hidatsa Eagle Trapping* (1928), and *The Hidatsa Earthlodge*
(1934). *Buffalo Bird Woman's Garden* was Wilson's doctoral dissertation; its subti-
tle, *An Indian Interpretation,* reflects his commitment to personal narratives. In
addition, Wilson was perhaps the first anthropologist to make effective use of biography to express the culture he studied. Not only were *Goodbird the Indian: His
Story* (1914) and *Waheenee: An Indian Girl's Story* (the biography of Buffalo Bird
Woman, published in 1921) stories by Indians for non-Indians, but they also
showed the cultural changes and adaptations experienced by Buffalo Bird Woman's
family.[19] The bicultural adaptations of Goodbird and Wolf Chief provided the
window through which Wilson viewed the traditionalism of Buffalo Bird Woman.

By her own account, Buffalo Bird Woman was born about 1839, "in the
Awatixa Village" (Sakakawea), one of the three Hidatsa villages along the Knife
River.[20] She was about four years old when the Hidatsa moved to Like-a-fishhook
village, and there she grew to adulthood and middle age. She was the daughter
of Weahtee or Wants-to-be-a-woman and, according to Hidatsa custom, became
a member of Weahtee's clan, the Tsistska-doxpaka or Prairie Chicken clan. Also
by Hidatsa custom, Buffalo Bird Woman reckoned Weahtee and all her sisters col-
lectively as "mother," and she grew up under the cooperative tutelage of this cohe-
sive matrilineal household.[21] Buffalo Bird Woman's father, Small Ankle, was an
Awaxawi, a leading chief of that village group, member of the Midipadi or Water-
buster clan, and keeper of the clan's sacred bundle.

[17] Wilson to Wissler, June 14, 1916, American Museum of Natural History, New York.

[18] Wilson to Wissler, June 14, 1916.

[19] Schneider, in Goodbird, *Goodbird the Indian,* vii; Maxidiwiac, *Waheenee: An Indian Girl's
Story: Told by Herself to Gilbert L. Wilson* (St. Paul: Webb Publishing Co., 1921; Bismarck: State
Historical Society of North Dakota, 1981; Lincoln: University of Nebraska Press, Bison Books, 1981).

[20] Wilson, Field Report, 1908, vol. 7, p. 18, in Gilbert L. Wilson Papers, Minnesota Historical
Society.

[21] Maxidiwiac, *Waheenee,* 9. For a good discussion of Hidatsa matrilineal clans and kinship
arrangements, see Bowers, *Hidatsa Social and Ceremonial Organization,* 64–126.

Both Buffalo Bird Woman and Wolf Chief (who was born about 1849) were reared in the traditional Hidatsa manner at Like-a-fishhook village, and thus learned the practical techniques, roles, and values of their culture. While Wolf Chief incorporated the skills, knowledge, and values of traditionally male activities like hunting, horse training, eagle trapping, vision questing, and warring, Buffalo Bird Woman became a consummate agriculturist, earth-lodge builder, and mother. Each of them proved to be an indispensible source of knowledge on Hidatsa culture during the Like-a-fishhook years for Gilbert and Frederick Wilson. Both Buffalo Bird Woman and Wolf Chief had experienced dramatic changes. When Like-a-fishhook village was abandoned and reservation culture enveloped them, Buffalo Bird Woman was in her late forties, and Wolf Chief was in his late thirties. But as Hidatsa representatives of their respective genders, these two family members responded and adapted differently to the new life. For Wolf Chief, the disappearance of the buffalo, cessation of warfare, and suppression of traditional ceremonies meant an end to traditional male roles. New roles had to be substituted, and Wolf Chief made the transition as he learned to read and write the English language and eventually became a storekeeper. Role changes for Hidatsa women were not as radical. Buffalo Bird Woman, while trading the earthlodge for a log cabin, was able to continue many of her traditional activities, particularly those having to do with gardening. She never learned English, and she remained a staunch traditionalist until her death.[22]

Buffalo Bird Woman's Garden is a classic anthropological document on Indian agriculture. Buffalo Bird Woman provides deep and encompassing accounts of agricultural practices and related activities: methods of planting, harvesting, and other seasonal tasks; descriptions of food processing, cooking, and storing garden produce in well-built cache pits; the organization of women's work as it pertained to caring for household gardens; assisting neighbors during crucial periods of the agricultural cycle; the enculturation of young girls of the household into responsible adult female roles.

Hidatsa gardeners were sensitive to the ecological demands of the Northern Plains climate. They carved garden plots from wooded and brushy areas in fertile bottomlands, where tillable soil was renewed annually by flooding; they did not try to cultivate on the prairie, which was covered with dry, virtually impenetrable sod. Brush cleared for planting was spread over the plots and burned, for it was conventional wisdom that burning trees and brush "softened the soil and left it loose and mellow for planting" (p. 13). It also added nutrients to the soil. Corn was planted in hilled rows, with the hills approximately four feet apart, because "corn planted in hills too close together would have small ears and fewer of them" (p. 23). This spacing, wider than that used by today's corn farmers, may have been tuned to expected rainfall. Closer spacing would bring higher yields only if the growing season were unusually wet; wide spacing would bring acceptable yields

[22]Gilman and Schneider, *The Way to Independence*.

with normal or subnormal summer rainfall. This adjustment to conditions of low rainfall is consistent with the fact that one Hidatsa corn variety, flint, was well adapted to the semi-arid Northern Plains climate. It required only about sixty days to mature, was relatively resistant to hail and frost, and, because of its short stalk, withstood winds fairly well.[23] Another ecologically sound practice was fallowing, or taking a garden plot out of production for a number of years to let it rejuvenate. According to Buffalo Bird Woman, the Hidatsa normally fallowed for two years, and "Every one in the village knew the value of a two years' fallowing" (p. 114).[24] These ecological practices, as well as the Hidatsa settlement plan and village spatial relationships to adjacent environments, have been of immense interest to archaeologists, ethnologists, historians, and other scholars of Native American prehistoric and historic cultural adaptation. *Buffalo Bird Woman's Garden* remains one of the most detailed, in-depth accounts of aboriginal Native American agriculture ever published.

This book is also significant as a *woman's* account of traditional tribal life during the mid-1800s. The roles and contributions of Plains Indian women to tribal life went largely ignored by anthropologists of Wilson's generation. This ethnographic injustice resulted in the creation of false stereotypes pertaining to the life and lot of Plains Indian women which have only recently been challenged.[25] One cannot read *Buffalo Bird Woman's Garden* without marveling at the array of technical skills which Hidatsa women developed and applied to everyday life: agriculture, architecture, construction, storage, crafts, and cooking constitute just a few of the dimensions of knowledge which Buffalo Bird Woman and other Hidatsa women contributed. Indeed, most of the distinctive characteristics of the Plains Village lifeway are attributable to the high profile of women's economic and social activities.

Whatever flaws appear in Wilson's work on Hidatsa culture stem predominantly from the fact that he was a product of his times. In the early 1900s, scholars and the lay public alike viewed American Indians as members of a vanishing race, destined by events to lose their culture. Anthropologists motivated by this erroneous view sought to record traditional tribal culture before it disappeared from the lives and memories of those who practiced it. They failed to see the flexibility and dynamism in Indian cultures, characteristics which did not sever the Hidatsa people from the past but rather linked them to it in new ways. Wilson was no exception. As anthropologist Mary Jane Schneider has observed, "his focus on earlier Indian life prevented him from seeing how Indians were adapting to white culture and, at the same time, maintaining as much tribal culture as possible under the circum-

[23] George F. Will and George E. Hyde, *Corn Among the Indians of the Upper Missouri* (St. Louis: William Harvey Miner Co., 1917; Lincoln: University of Nebraska Press, 1964), 73, 284.
[24] Fallowing was also described by Prince Maximilian for the Knife River villages in 1833–34, and it probably constituted a long-standing Hidatsa and Mandan custom. Maximilian's *Travels in the Interior of North America, 1832–1834* are vols. 22 and 23 in Reuben Gold Thwaites, ed., *Early Western Travels* (Cleveland: Arthur H. Clark, 1906).
[25] See, for example, Patricia Albers and Beatrice Medicine, *The Hidden Half: Studies of Plains Indian Women* (Washington, D.C.: University Press of America, 1983).

stances. Fortunately, because of his dedication and scholarship, Wilson wrote down whatever he was told, whether it fit his needs or not, and so he left us an unparalleled record of adaptation and adjustment."[26] In the final analysis, even though Wilson did not focus on Hidatsa culture change and adaptation, he made it possible for others to do so.

In *Buffalo Bird Woman's Garden,* there is very little material on agricultural activities that postdates the allotment of Hidatsa lands and the introduction of Euro-American farming techniques (briefly discussed in Chapter 12, "Since White Men Came"). But this is fitting for Buffalo Bird Woman; she loved the "old ways" and lamented their passing. One can glean from this book her feelings, but they are stated forthrightly in *Waheenee:*

> I am an old woman now. The buffaloes and black-tail deer are gone, and our Indian ways are almost gone. Sometimes I find it hard to believe that I ever lived them.
>
> My little son grew up in the white man's school. He can read books, and he owns cattle and has a farm. He is a leader among our Hidatsa people, helping teach them to follow the white man's road.
>
> He is kind to me. We no longer live in an earth lodge, but in a house with chimneys; and my son's wife cooks by a stove.
>
> But for me, I cannot forget our old ways.
>
> Often in summer I rise at daybreak and steal out to the cornfields; and as I hoe the corn I sing to it, as we did when I was young. No one cares for our corn songs now.
>
> Sometimes at evening I sit, looking out on the big Missouri. The sun sets, and dusk steals over the water. In the shadows I seem again to see our Indian village, with smoke curling upward from the earth lodges; and in the river's roar I hear the yells of the warriors, the laughter of little children as of old. It is but an old woman's dream. Again I see but shadows and hear only the roar of the river; and tears come into my eyes. Our Indian life, I know, is gone forever.[27]

It is difficult to say whether Buffalo Bird Woman or Wilson was responsible for this melancholy expression of these beliefs. Probably both were, and the statement reflects her feelings as recast by Wilson into what was then a conventional literary idiom. But let it be recorded that they were both wrong. There is continuity between then and now. Through agricultural change, the development of ranching, the Great Depression, world wars, and the building of the Garrison Dam which flooded the bottomlands of the Missouri, the Hidatsa people continue the struggle to balance traditional culture, language, and values with the needs of late

---

[26] In Goodbird, *Goodbird the Indian,* xxviii.
[27] Maxidiwiac, *Waheenee,* 175–76.

twentieth-century life. There is much that Buffalo Bird Woman would recognize. Contemporary Hidatsa culture is not the same as the Plains village culture of the "old days," but how much of *any* group's culture has remained unchanged over the last two centuries? *Buffalo Bird Woman's Garden* is not the end, but the beginning. It is a foundation, a viewpoint, and it presents a cultural relationship with nature that we can all appreciate and from which we can all derive benefit. This, above all else, might be its most telling contribution.

Jeffery R. Hanson

PREFACE

The field of primitive economic activity has been largely left unculti-
vated by both economists and anthropologists. The present study by
Mr. Gilbert L. Wilson is an attempt to add to the scanty knowledge
already at hand on the subject of the economic life of the American Indian.

The work was begun without theory or thesis, but solely with the
object of gathering available data from an old woman expert agriculturist
in one of the oldest agricultural tribes accessible to a student of the
University of Minnesota. That the study has unexpectedly revealed
certain varieties of maize of apparently great value to agriculture in the
semi-arid areas west of Minnesota is a cause of satisfaction to both Mr.
Wilson and myself. This fact again emphasizes the wisdom of research
work in our universities. When, now and then, such practical dollar-
and-cent results follow such purely scientific researches, the wonder is
that university research work is not generously endowed by businesses
which largely profit by these researches.

It is the intention of those interested in the anthropological work of
the University of Minnesota that occasional publications will be issued
by the University on anthropological subjects, although at present there
is no justification for issuing a consecutive series. The present study is
the second one in the anthropological field published by the University.
The earlier one is number 6 in the *Studies in the Social Sciences*, issued
March, 1916.

ALBERT ERNEST JENKS
Professor of Anthropology

Buffalo Bird Woman's Garden

HIDATSA ALPHABET

a	as	a	in	what
e	"	ai	"	air
i	"	i	"	pique
o	"	o	"	tone
u	"	u	"	rule
ä	"	a	"	father
ë	"	ey	"	they
ï	"	i	"	machine
ą	"	u	"	hut
ĕ	"	e	"	met
ĭ	"	i	"	tin
c	"	sh	"	shun
x	"	ch	"	machen (German)
j	"	ch	"	mich (German)
z	"	z	"	azure

b, d, h, k, l, m, n, p, r, s, t, w, as in English
b, w, interchangeable with m
n, l, r, interchangeable with d

An apostrophe (') marks a short,
    nearly inaudible breathing.

Native Hidatsa words in this thesis are written in the foregoing alphabet. This does not apply to the tribal names Hidatsa, Mandan, Dakota, Arikara, Minitari.

AGRICULTURE OF THE HIDATSA INDIANS
AN INDIAN INTERPRETATION

FOREWORD

The Hidatsas, called Minitaris by the Mandans, are a Siouan linguistic tribe. Their language is closely akin to that of the Crows with whom they claim to have once formed a single tribe; a separation, it is said, followed a quarrel over a slain buffalo.

The name Hidatsa was formerly borne by one of the tribal villages. The other villages consolidated with it, and the name was adopted as that of the tribe. The name is said to mean "willows," and it was given the village because the god Itsikama'hidic promised that the villagers should become as numerous as the willows of the Missouri river.

Tradition says that the tribe came from Miniwakan, or Devils Lake, in what is now North Dakota; and that migrating west, they met the Mandans at the mouth of the Heart River. The two tribes formed an alliance and attempted to live together as one people. Quarrels between their young men caused the tribes to separate, but the Mandans loyally aided their friends to build new villages a few miles from their own. How long the two tribes dwelt at the mouth of the Heart is not known. They were found there with the Arikaras about 1765. In 1804 Lewis and Clark found the Hidatsas in three villages at the mouth of the Knife River, and the Mandans in two villages a few miles lower down on the Missouri.

In 1832 the artist Catlin visited the two tribes, remaining with them several months. A year later Maximilian of Wied visited them with the artist Bodmer. Copies of Bodmer's sketches, in beautiful lithograph, are found in the library of the Minnesota Historical Society. Catlin's sketches, also in lithograph, are in the Minneapolis Public Library.

Smallpox nearly exterminated the Mandans in 1837-8, not more than 150 persons surviving. The same epidemic reduced the Hidatsas to about 500 persons. The remnants of the two tribes united and in 1845 removed up the Missouri and built a village at Like-a-fishhook bend close to the trading post of Fort Berthold. They were joined by the Arikaras in 1862. Neighboring lands were set apart as a reservation for them; and there the three tribes, now settled on allotments, still dwell.

The Mandans and Hidatsas have much intermarried. By custom children speak usually the language of their mother, but understand perfectly the dialect of either tribe.

In 1877 Washington Matthews, for several years government physician to the Fort Berthold Reservation Indians, published a short description of

Hidatsa-Mandan culture and a grammar and vocabulary of the Hidatsa language.[1]   More extensive notes intended by him for publication were destroyed by fire.

In 1902 the writer was called to the pastorate of the Presbyterian church of Mandan, North Dakota.   In ill health, he was advised by his physician to purchase pony and gun and seek the open; but spade and pick plied among the old Indian sites in the vicinity proved more interesting.   A considerable collection of archaeological objects was accumulated, a part of which now rests in the shelves of the Minnesota Historical Society; the rest will shortly be placed in the collections of the American Museum of Natural History.

In 1906 the writer and his brother, Frederick N. Wilson, an artist, and E. R. Steinbrueck drove by wagon from Mandan to Independence, Fort Berthold reservation.   The trip was made to obtain sketches for illustrating a volume of stories, since published.[2]   At Independence the party made the acquaintance of Edward Goodbird, his mother Maxi'diwiac, and the latter's brother Wolf Chief.   A friendship was thus begun which has been of the greatest value to the writer of this paper.

A year later Mr. George G. Heye sent the writer to Fort Berthold reservation to collect objects of Mandan-Hidatsa culture.   Among those that were obtained was a rare old medicine shrine.   Description of this shrine and Wolf Chief's story of its origin have been published.[3]

In 1908 the writer and his brother, both now resident in Minneapolis, were sent by Dr. Clark Wissler, curator of anthropology, American Museum of Natural History, to begin cultural studies among the Hidatsas. This work, generously supported by the Museum, has been continued by the writer each succeeding summer.   His reports, preparations to edit which are now being made, will appear in the Museum's publications.

In February, 1910, the writer was admitted as a student in the Graduate School, University of Minnesota, majoring in Anthropology.   At suggestion of his adviser, Dr. Albert E. Jenks, and with permission of Dr. Wissler, he chose for his thesis subject, *Agriculture of the Hidatsa Indians: An Indian Interpretation.*   It was the adviser's opinion that such a study held promise of more than usual interest.   Most of the tribes in the eastern area of what is now the United States practiced agriculture.   It is well known that maize, potatoes, pumpkins, squashes, beans, sweet potatoes, cotton, tobacco, and other familiar plants were cultivated by Indians centuries before Columbus.   Early white settlers learned the value of the new

---

[1] Washington Matthews, *Ethnography and Philology of the Hidatsa Indians.*   U. S. Geological and Geographical Survey.

[2] Gilbert L. Wilson, *Myths of the Red Children.*   Ginn and Company, 1907.

[3] George H. Pepper and Gilbert L. Wilson, *An Hidatsa Shrine and the Beliefs Respecting It.*   Memoirs of the American Anthropological Association, 1908.

food plants, but have left us meager accounts of the native methods of tillage; and the Indians, driven from the fields of their fathers, became roving hunters; or adopting iron tools, forgot their primitive implements and methods. The Hidatsas and Mandans, shut in their stockaded villages on the Missouri by the hostile Sioux, were not able to abandon their fields if they would. Living quite out of the main lines of railroad traffic, they remained isolated and with culture almost unchanged until about 1885, when their village at Fort Berthold was broken up. It seemed probable that a carefully prepared account of Hidatsa agriculture might very nearly describe the agriculture practiced by our northern tribes in pre-Columbian days. It was hoped that this thesis might be such an account.

But the writer is a student of anthropology; and his interest in the preparation of his thesis could not be that of an agriculturist. The question arose at the beginning of his labors, Shall the materials of this thesis be presented as a study merely in primitive agriculture, or as a phase of material culture interpreting something of the inner life, of the soul, of an Indian? It is the latter aim that the writer endeavors to accomplish.

But again came up a question, By what plan may this best be done? The more usual way would be to collect exhaustively facts from available informants; sift from them those facts that are typical and representative; and present these, properly grouped, with the collector's interpretation of them. But for his purpose and aim, it has seemed to the writer that the type choice should be human; that is, instead of seeking typical facts from multiple sources, he should rather seek a typical informant, a representative agriculturist—presumably a woman—of the Indian group to be studied, and let the informant interpret her agricultural experiences in her own way. We might thus expect to learn how much one Indian woman knew of agriculture; what she did as an agriculturist and what were her motives for doing; and what proportion of her thought and labor were given to her fields.

After consulting both Indians and whites resident on the reservation, the writer chose for typical or representative informant, his interpreter's mother, Maxi'diwiac.

The writer's summer visit of 1912 to Fort Berthold Reservation was planned to obtain material for his thesis. His brother again accompanied him, and for the expenses of the trip a grant of $500 was made by Curator Wissler. This trip the writer will remember as one of the pleasantest experiences of his life. The generous interest of Dr. Jenks and Dr. Wissler in his plans was equaled by the faithful coöperation of interpreter and informant. The writer and his brother arrived at the reservation in the beginning of corn harvest. As already stated, Maxi'diwiac was the principal informant, and her account was taken down almost literally as translated by Goodbird. Models of tools, drying stage, and other objects pertaining to agriculture were made and photographed, and sketched. Before the harvest closed notes were obtained which furnished the material for the greater part of this thesis.

In the summers of 1913, 1914, and 1915, additional matter was recovered. Previously written notes were read to Maxi'diwiac and corrections made.

In addition to the museum's annual grant of $250, Dean A. F. Woods, Department of Agriculture, University of Minnesota, in 1914 contributed $60 for photographing, and collecting specimens of Hidatsa corn; and Mr. M. L. Wilson of the Agricultural Experiment Station, Bozeman, Montana, obtained for the writer a grant of $50 for like purposes.

A few words should now be said of informant and interpreter. Maxi'-diwiac, or Buffalobird-woman, is a daughter of Small Ankle, a leader of the Hidatsas in the trying time of the tribe's removal to what is now Fort Berthold reservation. She was born on one of the villages at Knife River two years after the "smallpox year," or about 1839. She is a conservative and sighs for the good old times, yet is aware that the younger generation of Indians must adopt civilized ways. Ignorant of English, she has a quick intelligence and a memory that is marvelous. To her patience and loyal interest is chiefly due whatever of value is in this thesis. In the sweltering heat of an August day she has continued dictation for nine hours, lying down but never flagging in her account, when too weary to sit longer in a chair. Goodbird's testimony that his mother "knows more about old ways of raising corn and squashes than any one else on this reservation," is not without probability. Until recently, a small part of Goodbird's plowed field was each year reserved for her, that she might plant corn and beans and squashes, cultivating them in old fashioned way, by hoe. Such corn, of her own planting and selection, has taken first prize at an agricultural fair, held recently by the reservation authorities.

Edward Goodbird, or Tsaka'kasakic, the writer's interpreter, is a son of Maxi'diwiac, born about November, 1869. Goodbird was one of the first of the reservation children to be sent to the mission school; and he is now native pastor of the Congregational chapel at Independence. He speaks the Hidatsa, Mandan, Dakota, and English languages. Goodbird is a natural student; and he has the rarer gift of being an artist. His sketches—and they are many—are crude; but they are drawn in true perspective and do not lack spirit. Goodbird's life, dictated by himself, has been recently published.[4]

Indians have the gentle custom of adopting very dear friends by relationship terms. By such adoption Goodbird is the writer's brother; Maxi'diwiac is his mother.

[4] Gilbert L. Wilson, *Goodbird, the Indian: His Story.* Fleming H. Revell Co. 1914.

For his part in the account of the *Agriculture of the Hidatsa Indians*, the writer claims no credit beyond arranging the material and putting the interpreter's Indian-English translations into proper idiom. Bits of Indian philosophy and shrewd or humorous observations found in the narrative are not the writer's, but the informant's, and are as they fell from her lips. The writer has sincerely endeavored to add to the narrative essentially nothing of his own.

Agriculture of the Hidatsa Indians is not, then, an account merely of Indian agriculture. It is an Indian woman's interpretation of economics; the thoughts she gave to her fields; the philosophy of her labors. May the Indian woman's story of her toil be a plea for our better appreciation of her race.

CHAPTER I

TRADITION

We Hidatsas believe that our tribe once lived under the waters of Devils Lake. Some hunters discovered the root of a vine growing downward; and climbing it, they found themselves on the surface of the earth. Others followed them, until half the tribe had escaped; but the vine broke under the weight of a pregnant woman, leaving the rest prisoners. A part of our tribe are therefore still beneath the lake.

My father, Small Ankle, going, when a young man, on a war party, visited Devils Lake. "Beneath the waves," he said, "I heard a faint drumming, as of drums in a big dance." This story is true; for Sioux, who now live at Devils Lake, have also heard this drumming.

Those of my people who escaped from the lake built villages near by. These were of earth lodges, such as my tribe built until very recent years; two such earth lodges are still standing on this reservation.

The site where an earth lodge has stood is marked by an earthen ring, rising about what was once the hard trampled floor. There are many such earthen rings on the shores of Devils Lake, showing that, as tradition says, our villages stood there. There were three of these villages, my father said, who several times visited the sites.

Near their villages, the people made gardens; and in these they planted ground beans and wild potatoes, from seed brought with them from their home under the water. These vegetables we do not cultivate now; but we do gather them in the fall, in the woods along the Missouri where they grow wild. They are good eating.

These gardens by Devils Lake I think must have been rather small. I know that in later times, whenever my tribe removed up the Missouri to build a new village, our fields, the first year, were quite small; for clearing the wooded bottom land was hard work. A family usually added to their clearing each year, until their garden was as large as they cared to cultivate.

As yet, my people knew nothing of corn or squashes. One day a war party, I think of ten men, wandered west to the Missouri River. They saw on the other side a village of earth lodges like their own. It was a village of the Mandans. The villagers saw the Hidatsas, but like them, feared to cross over, lest the strangers prove to be enemies.

It was autumn, and the Missouri River was running low so that an arrow could be shot from shore to shore. The Mandans parched some ears of ripe corn with the grain on the cob; they broke the ears in pieces, thrust the pieces on the points of arrows, and shot them across the river. "Eat!" they said, whether by voice or signs, I do not know. The word for "eat" is the same in the Hidatsa and Mandan languages.

The warriors ate of the parched corn, and liked it. They returned to their village and said, "We have found a people living by the Missouri River who have a strange kind of grain, which we ate and found good!" The tribe was not much interested and made no effort to seek the Mandans, fearing, besides, that they might not be friendly.

However, a few years after, a war party of the Hidatsas crossed the Missouri and visited the Mandans at their village near Bird Beak Hill. The Mandan chief took an ear of yellow corn, broke it in two, and gave half to the Hidatsas. This half-ear the Hidatsas took home, for seed; and soon every family was planting yellow corn.

I think that seed of other varieties of corn, and of beans, squashes, and sunflowers, were gotten of the Mandans[1] afterwards; but there is no story telling of this, that I know.

I do not know when my people stopped planting ground beans and wild potatoes; but ground beans are hard to dig, and the people, anyway, liked the new kind of beans better.

Whether the ground beans and wild potatoes of the Missouri bottoms are descended from the seed planted by the villagers at Devils Lake, I do not know.

My tribe, as our old men tell us, after they got corn, abandoned their villages at Devils Lake, and joined the Mandans near the mouth of the Heart River. The Mandans helped them build new villages here, near their own. I think this was hundreds of years ago.

Firewood growing scarce, the two tribes removed up the Missouri to the mouth of the Knife River, where they built the Five Villages, as they called them. Smallpox was brought to my people here, by traders. In a single year, more than half my tribe died, and of the Mandans, even more.

Those who survived removed up the Missouri and built a village at Like-a-fishhook bend, where they lived together, Hidatsas and Mandans, as one tribe. This village we Hidatsas called Mu'a-idu'skupe-hi'cec, or

[1] "In the garden vegetable family are five; corn, beans, squashes, sunflowers, and tobacco. The seeds of all these plants were brought up from beneath the ground by the Mandan people.

"Now the corn, as we believe, has an enemy—the sun who tries to burn the corn. But at night, when the sun has gone down, the corn has magic power. It is the corn that brings the night moistures—the early morning mist and fog, and the dew—as you can see yourself in the morning from the water dripping from the corn leaves. Thus the corn grows and keeps on until it is ripe.

"The sun may scorch the corn and try hard to dry it up, but the corn takes care of itself, bringing the moistures that make the corn, and also the beans, sunflowers, squashes, and tobacco grow.

"The corn possesses all this magic power.

"When you white people met our Mandan people we gave to the whites the name Maci', or Waci', meaning nice people, or pretty people. We called them by this name because they had white faces and wore fine clothes. We said also 'We will call these people our friends!' And from that time to this we have never made war on white men.

"Our Mandan corn must now be all over the world, for we gave the white men our seeds. And so it seems we Mandans have helped every people. But the seed of our varieties of corn were originally ours.

"We know that white men must also have had corn seed, for their corn is different from ours. But all we older folk can tell our native corn from that of white men."—WOUNDED FACE (Mandan)

Like-a-fishhook village, after the bend on which it stood; but white men called it Fort Berthold, from a trading post that was there.

We lived in Like-a-fishhook village about forty years, or until 1885, when the government began to place families on allotments.

The agriculture of the Hidatsas, as I now describe it, I saw practiced in the gardens of Like-a-fishhook village, in my girlhood, before my tribe owned plows.

CHAPTER II

BEGINNING A GARDEN

Turtle

My great-grandmother, as white men count their kin, was named Atą'kic, or Soft-white Corn. She adopted a daughter, Mata'tic, or Turtle. Some years after, a daughter was born to Atą'kic, whom she named Otter.

Turtle and Otter both married. Turtle had a daughter named Ica'wikec, or Corn Sucker;[1] and Otter had three daughters, Want-to-be-a-woman, Red Blossom, and Strikes-many-women, all younger than Corn Sucker.

The smallpox year at Five Villages left Otter's family with no male members to support them. Turtle and her daughter were then living in Otter's lodge; and Otter's daughters, as Indian custom bade, called Corn Sucker their elder sister.

It was a custom of the Hidatsas, that if the eldest sister of a household married, her younger sisters were also given to her husband, as they came of marriageable age. Left without male kin by the smallpox, my grandmother's family was hard put to it to get meat; and Turtle gladly gave her daughter to my father, Small Ankle, whom she knew to be a good hunter. Otter's daughters, reckoned as Corn Sucker's sisters, were given to Small Ankle as they grew up; the eldest, Want-to-be-a-woman, was my mother.

When I was four years old, my tribe and the Mandans came to Like-a-fishhook bend. They came in the spring and camped in tepees, or skin tents. By Butterfly's winter count, I know they began building earth lodges the next winter. I was too young to remember much of this.

Two years after we came to Like-a-fishhook bend, smallpox again visited my tribe; and my mother, Want-to-be-a-woman, and Corn Sucker, died of it. Red Blossom and Strikes-many-women survived, whom I now called my mothers. Otter and old Turtle lived with us; I was taught to call them my grandmothers.

Clearing Fields

Soon after they came to Like-a-fishhook bend, the families of my tribe began to clear fields, for gardens, like those they had at Five Villages. Rich black soil was to be found in the timbered bottom lands of the Missouri. Most of the work of clearing was done by the women.

In old times we Hidatsas never made our gardens on the untimbered, prairie land, because the soil there is too hard and dry. In the bottom lands by the Missouri, the soil is soft and easy to work.

---

[1] Corn sucker, i. e., the extra shoot or stem that often springs up from the base of the maize plant.

9

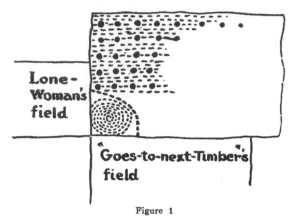

Figure 1

Map of newly broken field drawn under Buffalobird-woman's direction. The heavy dots represent corn hills; the dashes, the clearing and breaking of ground between, done after hills were planted.

In the lower left hand corner is the ground that was in dispute.

My mothers and my two grandmothers worked at clearing our family's garden. It lay east of the village at a place where many other families were clearing fields.

I was too small to note very much at first. But I remember that my father set boundary marks—whether wooden stakes or little mounds of earth or stones, I do not now remember—at the corners of the field we claimed. My mothers and my two grandmothers began at one end of this field and worked forward. All had heavy iron hoes, except Turtle, who used an old fashioned wooden digging stick.

With their hoes, my mothers cut the long grass that covered much of the field, and bore it off the line, to be burned. With the same implements, they next dug and softened the soil in places for the corn hills, which were laid off in rows. These hills they planted. Then all summer they worked with their hoes, clearing and breaking the ground between the hills.

Trees and bushes I know must have been cut off with iron axes; but I remember little of this, because I was only four years old when the clearing was begun.

I have heard that in very old times, when clearing a new field, my people first dug the corn hills with digging sticks; and afterwards, like my mothers, worked between the hills, with bone hoes. My father told me this.

Whether stone axes were used in old times to cut the trees and under-growths, I do not know. I think fields were never then laid out on ground that had large trees on it.

Dispute and Its Settlement

About two years after the first ground was broken in our field, a dispute I remember, arose between my mothers and two of their neighbors, Lone Woman and Goes-to-next-timber.

These two women were clearing fields adjoining that of my mothers; as will be seen by the accompanying map (figure 1), the three fields met at a corner. I have said that my father, to set up claim to his field, had placed marks, one of them in the corner at which met the fields of Lone Woman and Goes-to-next-timber; but while my mothers were busy clearing and digging up the other end of their field, their two neighbors invaded this marked-off corner; Lone Woman had even dug up a small part before she was discovered.

However, when they were shown the mark my father had placed, the two women yielded and accepted payment for any rights they might have.

It was our Indian rule to keep our fields very sacred. We did not like to quarrel about our garden lands. One's title to a field once set up, no one ever thought of disputing it; for if one were selfish and quarrelsome, and tried to seize land belonging to another, we thought some evil would come upon him, as that some one of his family would die. There is a story of a black bear who got into a pit that was not his own, and had his mind taken away from him for doing so!

Turtle Breaking Soil

Lone Woman and Goes-to-next-timber having withdrawn, my grandmother, Turtle, volunteered to break the soil of the corner that had been in dispute. She was an industrious woman. Often, when my mothers were busy in the earth lodge, she would go out to work in the garden, taking me with her for company. I was six years old then, I think, quite too little to help her any, but I liked to watch my grandmother work.

With her digging stick, she dug up a little round place in the center of the corner (figure 1); and circling around this from day to day, she gradually enlarged the dug-up space. The point of her digging stick she forced into the soft earth to a depth equal to the length of my hand, and pried up the soil. The clods she struck smartly with her digging stick, sometimes with one end, sometimes with the other. Roots of coarse grass, weeds, small brush and the like, she took in her hand and shook, or struck them against the ground, to knock off the loose earth clinging to them; she then cast them into a little pile to dry.

In this way she accumulated little piles, scattered rather irregularly over the dug-up ground, averaging, perhaps, four feet, one from the other. In a few days these little piles had dried; and Turtle gathered them up into a heap, about four feet high, and burned them, sometimes within the cleared ground, sometimes a little way outside.

In the corner that had been in dispute, and in other parts of the field, my grandmother worked all summer. I do not remember how big our garden was at the end of her summer's work, nor how many piles of roots she burned; but I remember distinctly how she put the roots of weeds and grass and brush into little piles to dry, which she then gathered into heaps and burned. She did not attempt to burn over the whole ground, only the heaps.

Afterwards, we increased our garden from year to year until it was as large as we needed. I remember seeing my grandmother digging along the edges of the garden with her digging stick, to enlarge the field and make the edges even and straight.

I remember also, that as Turtle dug up a little space, she would wait until the next season to plant it. Thus, additional ground dug up in the summer or fall would be planted by her the next spring.

There were two or three elm trees in the garden; these my grandmother left standing.

It must not be supposed that upon Turtle fell all the work of clearing

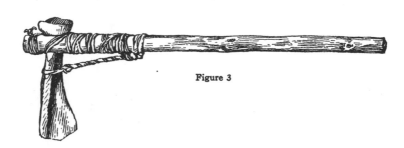

Figure 3

Figure 2. Drawn from specimen in author's collection. Length of specimen, 37½ inches.

Figure 3. Drawn from model made by Buffalobird-woman, duplicating that used by her grandmother. Specimen is of full size. Length of wooden handle, 35 inches; length of bone blade, 8½ inches. The blade is made of the shoulder bone of an ox.

land to enlarge our garden; but she liked to have me with her when she worked, and I remember best what I saw her do. As I was a little girl then, I have forgotten much that she did; but this that I have told, I remember distinctly.

Fig. 2

Turtle's Primitive Tools

In breaking ground for our garden, Turtle always used an ash digging stick (figure 2); and when hoeing time came, she hoed the corn with a bone hoe (figure 3). Digging sticks are still used in my tribe for digging wild turnips; but even in my grandmother's lifetime, digging sticks and bone hoes, as garden tools, had all but given place to iron hoes and axes.

My grandmother was one of the last women of my tribe to cling to these old fashioned implements. Two other women, I remember, owned bone hoes when I was a little girl; but Turtle, I think, was the very last one in the tribe who actually worked in her garden with one.

This hoe my grandmother kept in the lodge, under her bed; and when any of the children of the household tried to get it out to look at it, she would cry, "Let that hoe alone; you will break it!"

Beginning a Field in Later Times

As I grew up, I learned to work in the garden, as every Hidatsa woman was expected to learn; but iron axes and hoes, bought of the traders, were now used by everybody, and the work of clearing and breaking a new field was less difficult than it had been in our grandfathers' times. A family had also greater freedom in choosing where they should have their garden, since with iron axes they could more easily cut down any small trees and bushes that might be on the land. However, to avoid having to cut down big trees, a rather open place was usually chosen.

A family, then, having chosen a place for a field, cleared off the ground as much as they could, cutting down small trees and bushes in such way that the trees fell all in one direction. Some of the timber that was fit might be taken home for firewood; the rest was let lie to dry until spring, when it was fired. The object of felling the trees in one direction was to make them cover the ground as much as possible, since firing them softened the soil and left it loose and mellow for planting. We sought always to burn over all the ground, if we could.

Before firing, the family carefully raked off the dry grass and leaves from the edge of the field, and cut down any brush wood. This was done that the fire might not spread to the surrounding timber, nor out on the prairie. Prairie fires and forest fires are even yet not unknown on our reservation.

Planting season having come, the women of the household planted the field in corn. The hills were in rows, and about four feet or a little less apart. They were rather irregularly placed the first year. It was easy to make a hill in the ashes where a brush heap had been fired, or in soil that was free of roots and stumps; but there were many stumps in the field, left over from the previous summer's clearing. If the planter found a stump stood where a hill should be, she placed the hill on this side the stump or beyond it, no matter how close this brought the hill to the next in the row. Thus, the corn hills did not stand at even distances in the row the first year; but the rows were always kept even and straight.

While the corn was coming up, the women worked at clearing out the roots and smaller stumps between the hills; but a stump of any considerable size was left to rot, especially if it stood midway between two corn hills, where it did not interfere with their cultivation.

My mothers and I used to labor in a similar way to enlarge our fields. With our iron hoes we made hills along the edge of the field and planted corn; then, as we had opportunity, we worked with our hoes between the corn hills to loosen up the soil.

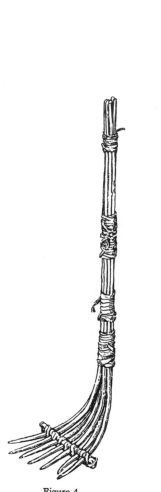

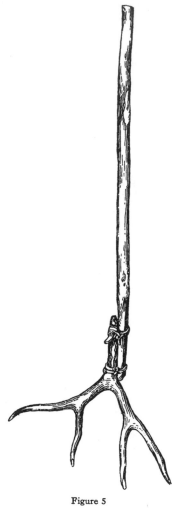

Figure 4

Drawn from specimen made by Yellow Hair. Length of specimen, following curvature of tines, 36½ inches.

Figure 5

Drawn from specimen made by Buffalobird-woman. Length of wooden handle, 42 inches; spread of tines of antler, 15½ inches.

Although our tribe now had iron axes and hoes from the traders, they still used their native made rakes. These were of wood (figure 4), or of the antler of a black-tailed deer (figure 5). It was with such rakes that the edges of a newly opened field were cleaned of leaves for the firing of the brush, in the spring.

Trees in the Garden

Trees were not left standing in the garden, except perhaps one to shade the watchers' stage. If a tree stood in the field, it shaded the corn; and that on the north side of the tree never grew up strong, and the stalks would be yellow.

Cottonwood trees were apt to grow up in the field, unless the young shoots were plucked up as they appeared.

Our West Field

The field which Turtle helped to clear, lay, I have said, east of the village. I was about nineteen years old, I think, when my mothers determined to clear ground for a second field, west of the village.

There were five of us who undertook the work, my father, my two mothers, Red Blossom and Strikes-many-women, my sister, Cold Medicine, and myself. We began in the fall, after harvesting the corn from our east garden, so that we had leisure for the work; we had been too busy to begin earlier in the season.

We chose a place down in the bottoms, overgrown with willows; and with our axes we cut the willows close to the ground, letting them lie as they fell.

I do not know how many days we worked; but we stopped when we had cleared a field of about seventy-five by one hundred yards, perhaps. In our east, or yellow corn field, we counted nine rows of corn to one *na'xu;* and I remember that when we came to plant our new field, it had nine *na'xu.*

Burning Over the Field

The next spring my father, his two wives, my sister and I went out and burned the felled willows and brush which the spring sun had dried. We did not burn them every day; only when the weather was fine. We would go out after breakfast, burn until tired of the work, and come home.

We sought to burn over the whole field, for we knew that this left a good, loose soil. We did not pile the willows in heaps, but loosened them from the ground or scattered them loosely but evenly over the soil. In some places the ground was quite bare of willows; but we collected dry grass and weeds and dead willows, and strewed them over these bare places, so that the fire would run over the whole area of the field.

It took us about four days to burn over the field.

It was well known in my tribe that burning over new ground left the soil soft and easy to work, and for this reason we thought it a wise thing to do.

CHAPTER III

SUNFLOWERS

Remark by Maxi'diwiac

This that I am going to tell you of the planting and harvesting of our crops is out of my own experience, seen with my own eyes. In olden times, I know, my tribe used digging sticks and bone hoes for garden tools; and I have described how I saw my grandmother use them. There may be other tools or garden customs once in use in my tribe, and now forgotten; of them I cannot speak. There were families in Like-a-fishhook village less industrious than ours, and some families may have tilled their fields in ways a little different; of them, also, I can not speak. This that I now tell is as I saw my mothers do, or did myself, when I was young. My mothêrs were industrious women, and our family had always good crops; and I will tell now how the women of my father's family cared for their fields, as I saw them, and helped them.

Planting Sunflowers

The first seed that we planted in the spring was sunflower seed. Ice breaks on the Missouri about the first week in April; and we planted sunflower seed as soon after as the soil could be worked. Our native name for the lunar month that corresponds most nearly to April, is Mapi'-o'cĕ-mi'di, or Sunflower-planting-moon.

Planting was done by hoe, or the woman scooped up the soil with her hands. Three seeds were planted in a hill, at the depth of the second joint of a woman's finger. The three seeds were planted together, pressed into the loose soil by a single motion, with thumb and first two fingers. The hill was heaped up and patted firm with the palm in the same way as we did for corn.

Usually we planted sunflowers only around the edges of a field. The hills were placed eight or nine paces apart; for we never sowed sunflowers thickly. We thought a field surrounded thus by a sparce-sown row of sunflowers, had a handsome appearance.

Sometimes all three seeds sprouted and came up together; sometimes only two sprouted; sometimes one.

Varieties

Of cultivated sunflowers we had several varieties, black, white, red, striped, named from the color of the seed. The varieties differed only in color; all had the same taste and smell, and were treated alike in cooking.

White sunflower seed when pounded into meal, turned dark, but I think this was caused by the parching.

Each family raised the variety they preferred. The varieties were well fixed; black seed produced black; white seed, white.

Harvesting the Seed

Although our sunflower seed was the first crop to be planted in the spring, it was the last to be harvested in the fall.

For harvesting, we reckoned two kinds of flowers, or heads.

A stalk springing from seed of one of our cultivated varieties had one, sometimes two, or even three larger heads, heavy and full, bending the top of the stalk with their weight of seed. Some of these big heads had each a seed area as much as eleven inches across; and yielded each an even double handful of seed. We called the seed from these big heads mapi'-i'ti'a from mapi', sunflower, or sunflower seed, and i'ti'a, big.

Besides these larger heads, there were other and smaller heads on the stalk; and wild sunflowers bearing similar small heads grew in many places along the Missouri, and were sure to be found springing up in abandoned gardens. These smaller heads of the cultivated, and the heads of the wild, plants, were never more than five inches across; and these and their seed we called mapi'-na'ka, sunflower's child or baby sunflower.

Our sunflowers were ready for harvesting when the little petals that covered the seeds fell off, exposing the ripe seeds beneath. Also, the back of the head turned yellow; earlier in the season it would be green.

To harvest the larger heads, I put a basket on my back, and knife in hand, passed from plant to plant, cutting off each large head close to the stem; the severed heads I tossed into my basket. These heads I did not let dry on the stalk, as birds would devour the seeds.

My basket filled, I returned to the lodge, climbed the ladder to the roof, and spread the sunflower heads upon the flat part of the roof around the smoke hole, to dry. The heads were laid face downward, with the backs to the sun. When I was a girl, only three or four earth lodges in the village had peaked roofs; and these lodges were rather small. All the larger and better lodges, those of what we deemed wealthier families, were built with the top of the roof flat, like a floor. A flat roof was useful to dry things on; and when the weather was fair, the men often sat there and gossiped.

The sunflower heads were dried face downward, that the sun falling on the back of the head might dry and shrink the fiber, thus loosening the seeds. The heads were laid flat on the bare roof, without skins or other protection beneath. If a storm threatened, the unthreshed heads were gathered up and borne into the lodge; but they were left on the roof overnight, if the weather was fair.

When the heads had dried about four days, the seeds were threshed out; and I would fetch in from the garden another supply of heads to dry and thresh.

Threshing

To thresh the heads, a skin was spread and the heads laid on it face downward, and beaten with a stick. Threshing might be on the ground, or on the flat roof, as might be convenient.

An average threshing filled a good sized basket, with enough seed left over to make a small package.

Harvesting the Mapi'-na'ka

The smaller heads of the cultivated plants were sometimes gathered, dried, and threshed, as were the larger heads; but if the season was getting late and frost had fallen, and the seeds were getting loose in their pods, I more often threshed these smaller heads and those of the wild plants directly from the stalk.

For this I bore a carrying basket, swinging it around over my breast instead of my back; and going about the garden or into the places where the wild plants grew, I held the basket under these smaller, or baby sunflower heads, and beating them smartly with a stick, threshed the seeds into the basket. It took me about half a day to thresh a basket half full. The seeds I took home to dry, before sacking them.

The seeds from the baby sunflowers of both wild and cultivated plants were sacked together. The seeds of the large heads were sacked separately; and in the spring, when we came to plant, our seed was always taken from the sack containing the harvest of the larger heads.

In my father's family, we usually stored away two, sometimes three sacks of dried sunflower seed for winter use. Sacks were made of skins, perhaps fourteen inches high and eight inches in diameter, on an average.

Sunflower harvest came after we had threshed our corn; and corn threshing was in the first part of October.

Effect of Frost

Because they were gathered later, the seeds of baby sunflowers were looked upon as a kind of second crop; and as I have said, they were kept apart from the earlier harvest, because seed for planting was selected from the larger and earlier gathered heads. Gathered thus late, this second crop was nearly always touched by the frost, even before the seeds were threshed from the stalks.

This frosting of the seeds had an effect upon them that we rather esteemed. We made a kind of oily meal from sunflower seed, by pounding them in a corn mortar; but meal made from seed that had been frosted, seemed more oily than that from seed gathered before frost fell. The freezing of the seeds seemed to bring the oil out of the crushed kernels.

This was well known to us. The large heads, left on the roof over night, were sometimes caught by the frost; and meal made from their seed was more oily than that from unfrosted seed. Sometimes we took the threshed seed out of doors and let it get frosted, so as to bring out this oiliness. Frosting the seeds did not kill them.

The oiliness brought out by the frosting was more apparent in the seeds of baby sunflowers than in seeds of the larger heads. Seeds of the latter seemed never to have as much oil in them as seeds of the baby sunflowers.

Parching the Seed

To make sunflower meal the seeds were first roasted, or parched. This was done in a clay pot, for iron pots were scarce in my tribe when I was young. The clay pot in use in my father's family was about a foot high and eight or nine inches in diameter, as you see from measurements I make with my hands.

This pot I set on the lodge fire, working it down into the coals with a rocking motion, and raked coals around it; the mouth I tipped slightly toward me. I threw into the pot two or three double-handfuls of the seeds and as they parched, I stirred them with a little stick, to keep them from burning. Now and then I took out a seed and bit it; if the kernel was soft and gummy, I knew the parching was not done; but when it bit dry and crisp, I knew the seeds were cooked and I dipped them out with a horn spoon into a wooden bowl.

Again I threw into the pot two or three double-handfuls of seed to parch; and so, until I had enough.

As the pot grew quite hot I was careful not to touch it with my hands. The parching done, I lifted the pot out, first throwing over it a piece of old tent cover to protect my two hands.

Parching the seeds caused them to crack open somewhat.

The parched seeds were pounded in the corn mortar to make meal. Pounding sunflower seeds took longer, and was harder work, than pounding corn.

Four-vegetables-mixed

Sunflower meal was used in making a dish that we called do′patsa-makihi′kĕ, or four-vegetables-mixed; from do′patsa, four things; and makihi′kĕ, mixed or put together. Four-vegetables-mixed we thought our very best dish.

To make this dish, enough for a family of five, I did as follows:

I put a clay pot with water on the fire.

Into the pot I threw one double-handful of beans. This was a fixed quantity; I put in just one double-handful whether the family to be served was large or small; for a larger quantity of beans in this dish was apt to make gas on one's stomach.

When we dried squash in the fall we strung the slices upon strings of twisted grass, each seven Indian fathoms long; an Indian fathom is the distance between a woman's two hands outstretched on either side. From one of these seven-fathom strings I cut a piece as long as from my elbow to the tip of my thumb; the two ends of the severed piece I tied together, making a ring; and this I dropped into the pot with the beans.

When the squash slices were well cooked I lifted them out of the pot by the grass string into a wooden bowl. With a horn spoon I chopped and mashed the cooked squash slices into a mass, which I now returned to the pot with the beans. The grass string I threw away.

Figure 6

Drawn from specimens in author's collection.

To the mess I now added four or five double-handfuls of mixed meal, of pounded parched sunflower seed and pounded parched corn. The whole was boiled for a few minutes more, and was ready for serving.

I have already told how we parched sunflower seed; and that I used two or three double-handfuls of seed to a parching. I used two parchings of sunflower seed for one mess of four-vegetables-mixed. I also used two parchings of corn; but I put more corn into the pot at a parching than I did of sunflower seed.

Pounding the parched corn and sunflower seed reduced their bulk so that the four parchings, two of sunflower seed and two of corn, made but four or five double-handfuls of the mixed meal.

Four-vegetables-mixed was eaten freshly cooked; and the mixed corn-and-sunflower meal was made fresh for it each time. A little alkali salt might be added for seasoning, but even this was not usual. No other seasoning was used. Meat was not boiled with the mess, as the sunflower seed gave sufficient oil to furnish fat.

Four-vegetables-mixed was a winter food; and the squash used in its making was dried, sliced squash, never green, fresh squash.

The clay pot used for boiling this and other dishes was about the size of an iron dinner pot, or even larger. For a large family, the pot might be as much as thirteen or fourteen inches high. I have described that in use in my father's family.

When a mess of four-vegetables-mixed was cooked, I did not remove the pot from the coals, but dipped out the vegetables with a mountain-sheep horn spoon, into wooden bowls (figure 6.)

Sunflower-seed Balls

Sunflower meal of the parched seeds was also used to make sunflower seed balls; these were important articles of diet in olden times, and had a particular use.

For sunflower-seed balls I parched the seeds in a pot in the usual way, put them in a corn mortar and pounded them. When they were reduced to a fine meal I reached into the mortar and took out a handful of the meal, squeezing it in the fingers and palm of my right hand. This squeezing it made it into a kind of lump or ball.

This ball I enclosed in the two palms and gently shook it. The shaking brought out the oil of the seeds, cementing the particles of the meal and making the lump firm. I have said that frosted seeds gave out more oil than unfrosted; and that baby sunflower seeds gave out more oil than seeds from the big heads.

In olden times every warrior carried a bag of soft skin at his left side, supported by a thong over his right shoulder; in this bag he kept needles, sinews, awl, soft tanned skin for making patches for moccasins, gun caps, and the like. The warrior's powder horn hung on the outside of this bag.

In the bottom of this soft-skin bag the warrior commonly carried one of these sunflower-seed balls, wrapped in a piece of buffalo-heart skin. When worn with fatigue or overcome with sleep and weariness, the warrior took out his sunflower-seed ball, and nibbled at it to refresh himself. It was amazing what effect nibbling at the sunflower-seed ball had. If the warrior was weary, he began to feel fresh again; if sleepy, he grew wakeful.

Sometimes the warrior kept his sunflower-seed ball in his flint case that hung always at his belt over his right hip.

It was quite a general custom in my tribe for a warrior or hunter to carry one of these sunflower-seed balls.

We called the sunflower-seed ball mapi', the same name as for sunflower.

Sunflower meal, parched and pounded as described, was often mixed with corn balls, to which it gave an agreeable smell, as well as a pleasant taste.

CHAPTER IV

CORN

Planting

Corn planting began the second month after sunflower-seed was planted, that is in May; and it lasted about a month. It sometimes continued pretty well into June, but not later than that; for the sun then begins to go back into the south, and men began to tell eagle-hunting stories.

We knew when corn planting time came by observing the leaves of the wild gooseberry bushes. This bush is the first of the woods to leaf in the spring. Old women of the village were going to the woods daily to gather fire wood; and when they saw that the wild gooseberry bushes were almost in full leaf, they said, "It is time for you to begin planting corn!"

Corn was planted each year in the same hills.

Around each of the old and dead hills I loosened the soil with my hoe, first pulling up the old, dead roots of the previous year's plants; these dead roots, as they collected, were raked off with other refuse to one end of the field outside of the cultivated ground, to be burned.

This pulling up of the dead roots and working around the old hill with the hoe, left the soil soft and loose for the space of about eighteen inches in diameter; and in this soft soil I planted the corn in this manner:

I stooped over, and with fingers of both hands I raked away the loose soil for a bed for the seed; and with my fingers I even stirred the soil around with a circular motion to make the bed perfectly level so that the seeds would all lie at the same depth.

A small vessel, usually a wooden bowl, at my feet held the seed corn. With my right hand I took a small handful of the corn, quickly transferring half of it to my left hand; still stooping over, and plying both hands at the same time, I pressed the grains a half inch into the soil with my thumbs, planting two grains at a time, one with each hand.

I planted about six to eight grains in a hill[1] (figure 7). Then with my hands I raked the earth over the planted grains until the seed lay

[1] Buffalobird-woman says she planted six to eight kernels to a hill. Just what pattern she used she could not tell until she went out with a handful of seed and planted a few hills to revive her memory. The three patterns shown in figure 7 will show how she laid the grains in the bottom of the several hills.
—GILBERT L. WILSON

Figure 7

about the length of my fingers under the soil. Finally I patted the hill firm with my palms.

The space within the hill in which the seed kernels were planted should be about nine inches in diameter; but the completed hill should nearly cover the space broken up by the hoe.

The corn hills I planted well apart, because later, in hilling up, I would need room to draw earth from all directions over the roots to protect them from the sun, that they might not dry out. Corn planted in hills too close together would have small ears and fewer of them; and the stalks of the plants would be weak, and often dried out.

If the corn hills were so close together that the plants when they grew up, touched each other, we called them "smell-each-other"; and we knew that the ears they bore would not be plump nor large.

A Morning's Planting

We Hidatsa women were early risers in the planting season; it was my habit to be up before sunrise, while the air was cool, for we thought this the best time for garden work.

Having arrived at the field I would begin one hill, preparing it, as I have said, with my hoe; and so for ten rows each as long as from this spot to yonder fence—about thirty yards; the rows were about four feet apart, and the hills stood about the same distance apart in the row.

The hills all prepared, I went back and planted them, patting down each with my palms, as described. Planting corn thus by hand was slow work; but by ten o'clock the morning's work was done, and I was tired and ready to go home for my breakfast and rest; we did not eat before going into the field. The ten rows making the morning's planting contained about two hundred and twenty-five hills.

I usually went to the field every morning in the planting season, if the weather was fine. Sometimes I went out again a little before sunset and planted; but this was not usual.

Soaking the Seed

The very last corn that we planted we sometimes put into a little tepid water, if the season was late. Seed used for replanting hills that had been destroyed by crows or magpies we also soaked. We left the seed in the water only a short time, when the water was poured off.

The water should be tepid only, so that when poured through the fingers it felt hardly warmed. Hot water would kill the seeds.

Seed corn thus soaked would have sprouts a third of an inch long within four or five days after planting, if the weather was warm. I know this, because we sometimes dug up some of the seeds to see. This soaked seed produced strong plants, but the first-planted, dry seeds still produced the first ripened ears. .

If warm water was not convenient, I sometimes put these last planted corn seeds in my mouth; and when well wetted, planted them. But these mouth-wetted seeds produced, we thought, a great many wi'da-aka'ta, or goose-upper-roof-of-mouth, ears.

Planting for a Sick Woman

It was usual for the women of a household to do their own planting; but if a woman was sick, or for some reason was unable to attend to her planting, she sometimes cooked a feast, to which she invited the members of her age society and asked them to plant her field for her.

The members of her society would come upon an appointed day and plant her field in a short time; sometimes a half day was enough.

There were about thirty members in my age society when I was a young woman. If we were invited to plant a garden for some sick woman, each member would take a row to plant; and each would strive to complete her row first. A member having completed her row, might begin a second, and even a third row; or if, when each had completed one row, there was but a small part of the field yet unplanted, all pitched in miscellaneously and finished the planting.

Size of Our Biggest Field

When our corn was in, we began planting beans and squashes. Beans we commonly planted between corn rows, sometimes over the whole field, more often over a part of it. Our bean and squash planting I will describe later; and I speak of it now only because I wish to explain to you how a Hidatsa garden was laid out.

The largest field ever owned in my father's family was the one which I have said my grandmother Turtle helped clear, at Like-a-fishhook village, or Fort Berthold, as the whites called it. The field, begun small, was added to each year and did not reach its maximum size for some years.

The field was nearly rectangular in shape; at the time of its greatest size, its length was about equal to the distance from this spot to yonder fence—one hundred and eighty yards; and its width, to the distance from the corner of this cabin to yonder white post—ninety yards.

The size of a garden was determined chiefly by the industry of the family that owned it, and by the number of mouths that must be fed.

When I was six years old, there were, I think, ten in my father's family, of whom my two grandmothers, my mother and her three sisters, made six. I have said that my mother and her three sisters were wives of Small Ankle, my father. It was this year that my mother and Corn Sucker died, however.

My father's wives and my two grandmothers, all industrious women, added each year to the area of our field; for our family was growing. At the time our garden reached its maximum size, there were seven boys in the family; three of these died young, but four grew up and brought wives to live in our earth lodge.

Na'xu and Nu'cami

In our big garden at Like-a-fishhook village, nine rows of corn, running lengthwise with the field, made one na'xu, or Indian acre, as we usually

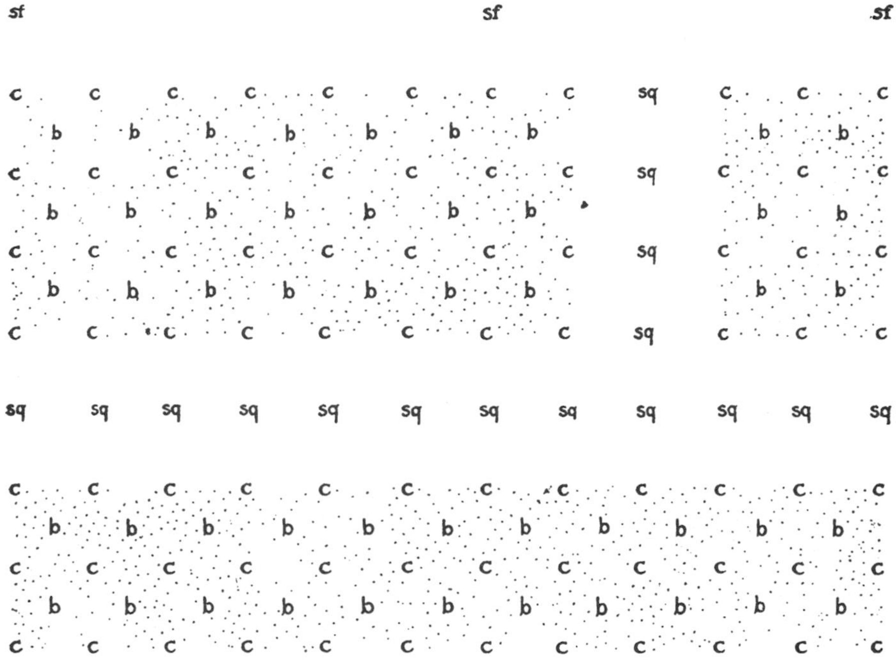

Figure 8

translate it. There were ten of these na'xus, or Indian acres, in the garden.

Some families of our village counted eight rows of corn to one na'xu, others counted ten rows.

The rows of the na'xus always ran the length of the garden; and if the field curved, as it sometimes did around a bend of the river, or other irregularity, the rows curved with it.

In our garden a row of squashes separated each na'xu from its neighbor.

Four rows of corn running widthwise with the garden made one nu'cami; and as was the na'xu, each nu'cami was separated from its neighbor by a row of squashes, or beans, or in some families, even by sunflowers.

Like those of the na'xus, the rows of the nu'camis often curved to follow some irregularity in the shape of the garden plot. (See figure 8.)

Hoeing

Hoeing time began when the corn was about three inches high; but this varied somewhat with the season. Some seasons were warm, and the corn and weeds grew rapidly; other seasons were colder, and delayed the growth of the corn.

Corn plants about three inches high we called "young-bird's-feather-tail-corn," because the plants then had blunt ends, like the tail feathers of a very young bird.

Corn and weeds alike grew rapidly now, and we women of the household were out with our hoes daily, to keep ahead of the weeds. We worked as in planting season, in the early morning hours.

I cultivated each hill carefully with my hoe as I came to it; and if the plants were small, I would comb the soil of the hill lightly with my fingers, loosening the earth and tearing out young weeds.

We did not hoe the corn alone, but went right through the garden, corn, squashes, beans, and all. Weeds were let lie on the ground, as they were now young and harmless.

We hoed but once, not very many weeds coming up to bother us afterwards. In my girlhood we were not troubled with mustard and thistles; these weeds have come in with white men.

In many families hoeing ended, I think, when the corn was about seven or eight inches high: but I remember when my mothers finished hoeing their big field at Like-a-fishhook village, the corn was about eighteen inches high, and the blossoms at the top of the plants were appearing.

A second hoeing began, it is true, when the corn silk appeared, but was accompanied by hilling, so that we looked upon it rather as a hilling time. Hilling was done to firm the plants against the wind and cover the roots from the sun. We hilled with earth, about four inches up around the roots of the corn.

Not a great many weeds were found in the garden at hilling time, unless the season had been wet; but weeds at this season are apt to have seeds, so that it was my habit to bear such weeds off the field, that the seeds might not fall and sprout the next season.

With the corn, the squashes and beans were also hilled; but this was an easier task. The bean hills, especially, were made small at the first, and hilling them up afterwards was not hard work. If beans were hilled too high the vines got beaten down into the mud by the rains and rotted.

The Watchers' Stage

Our corn fields had many enemies. Magpies, and especially crows, pulled up much of the young corn, so that we had to replant many hills. Crows were fond of pulling up the green shoots when they were a half inch or an inch high. Spotted gophers would dig up the seed from the roots of young plants. When the corn had eared, and the grains were still soft, blackbirds and crows were destructive.

Any hills of young corn that the birds destroyed, I replanted if the season was not too late. If only a part of the plants in a hill had been destroyed, I did not disturb the living plants, but replanted only the destroyed ones. In the place of each missing plant, I dug a little hole with my hand, and dropped in a seed.

We made scarecrows[2] to frighten the crows. Two sticks were driven into the ground for legs; to these were bound two other sticks, like outstretched arms; on the top was fastened a ball of cast-away skins, or the like, for a head. An old buffalo robe was drawn over the figure and a belt tied around its middle, to make it look like a man. Such a scarecrow would keep the crows away for a few days but when they saw that the figure never moved from its place, they lost their fear and returned.

A platform, or stage, was often built in a garden, where the girls and young women of the household came to sit and sing as they watched that crows and other thieves did not destroy the ripening crop. We cared for our corn in those days as we would care for a child; for we Indian people loved our gardens, just as a mother loves her children; and we thought that our growing corn liked to hear us sing, just as children like to hear their mother sing to them.[3] Also, we did not want the birds to come and steal our corn. Horses, too, might break in and crop the plants, or boys might steal the green ears and go off and roast them.

[2] "Twice in the corn season were scarecrows used; first, when the corn was just coming up; and again when the grain was forming on the ear and getting ripe."—EDWARD GOODBIRD

[3] In August, 1910, Buffalobird-woman related the story of "The Grandson," in the course of which she said in explanation of reference to a watchers' stage:

"I will now stop a moment to explain something in the other form of this tale.

"According to this way of telling it, there was a garden and in the middle of the garden was a tree. There was a platform under the tree made of trunks and slabs; and there those two girls sat to watch the garden and sing watch-garden songs. They did this to make the garden grow, just as people sing to a baby to make it be quiet and feel good. In old times we sang to a garden for a like reason, to make the garden feel good and grow. This custom was one used in every garden. Sometimes one or two women sang.

"The singing was begun in the spring and continued until the corn was ripe. We Indians loved our gardens and kept them clean; we did not let weeds grow in them. Always in every garden during the growing season, there would be some one working or singing.

"Now in old times, many of our gardens had resting stages, or watchers' stages, such as I have just described. We always made our gardens down in the woods by the river, because there is better ground there. When we cut off the timber we would often leave one tree standing in the garden. Under this tree were erected four forked posts, on which was laid a platform. This made the stage; in the tree overhead we often spread robes and blankets for shade.

"This resting stage was small. It was just big enough for two persons to sit on comfortably. Corn was never dried on it; it was used for a singing and resting place only. It was reached by a ladder. Its height was about four and a half feet high.

"This resting stage or watchers' stage was built on the north side of the tree so that the shade of the tree would fall upon it. Robes were laid on the floor of the stage to make a couch or bed. Sometimes people even slept on this platform—sometimes a man and his wife slept there.

"This resting stage we used to rest on after working in the garden; and to sing here the songs that we sang at this season of the year, and which I have called watch-garden songs. A place to cook in was not

Our Hidatsa name for such a stage was adukati' i'kakĕ-ma'tsati, or field watchers' stage; from adukati', field; i'kakĕ, watch; and ma'tsati, stage. These stages, while common, were not in every garden. I had one in my garden where I used to sit and sing.

A watchers' stage resembled a stage for drying grain, but it was built more simply. Four posts, forked at the top, supported two parallel beams, or stringers; on these beams was laid a floor of puncheons, or split small logs, at about the height of the full grown corn. This floor was about the length and breadth of Wolf Chief's table—forty-three by thirty-five inches— and was thus large enough to permit two persons to sit together. A ladder made of the trunk of a tree rested against the stage.

Such stages we did not value as we did our drying stages, nor did we use so much care in building them. If the posts were of green wood, we did not trouble to peel off the bark; at least, I never saw such posts with the bark peeled off. The beams in the forks of the posts often lay with the bark on. The puncheons that made the floor of the stage were free of bark, because they were commonly split from old, dead, floating logs, that we got down at the Missouri River; if the whole stage was built of these dead logs, as was often done, the bark would be wanting on every beam.

A watchers' stage, indeed, was usually of rather rough construction; wood was plentiful and easy to get, and the stage was rebuilt each year.

As I have said, it was our custom to locate our gardens on the timbered, bottom lands, and when we cleared off the timber and brush, we often left a tree, usually of cottonwood, standing in the field, to shade the watchers' stage. The stage stood on the north, or shady, side of the tree.

Cottonwood seedlings were apt to spring up in newly cleared ground. If there was no tree in the field, one of these seedlings might be let grow into a small tree. Cottonwoods grew very rapidly.

The tree that shaded the watchers' stage in our family field, and which I have indicated on the map, was about as high as my son Goodbird's cabin, and had a trunk about four inches in diameter. The cottonwood tree standing in Wolf Chief's corn field this present summer, is perhaps about the height of the trees that used to stand in our fields at Like-a-fish-hook village.

Explanation of Sketch of Watchers' Stage

My son Goodbird has made a sketch, under my direction, of a watchers' stage (figure 9).

far away on the edge of the garden. It was a kind of booth, or bower. With a stake we made holes in the ground in a circle, and into the holes thrust willows. The tops of these willows we bent toward the center and joined together to make a bower. Over the top we threw a robe. We built a fire beneath to cook by.

"Our gardens I am describing were those at Like-a-fishhook village; and they were on the Missouri on either side of the village. They were strung along the river bank for a mile or more on either side of the village."

The stage was placed close to the tree shading it, about a foot from the trunk.   Holes for the posts were dug with a long digging stick; and the posts were set firm, like fence posts.

The stage was made nearly square, so that the watchers could sit facing any side with equal ease.   The beams supporting the floor might be laid east and west, or north and south; but as the tree stood always on the south side of the stage, the floor beams lay always in one of these two ways.

Figure 9
Redrawn from sketch by Edward Goodbird.

In the sketch a skin[4] is seen lying on the stage floor.   This is a buffalo calf skin, folded fur out, to make a seat for the watcher.   The skin might be folded tail to head, or side to side; and sometimes it was folded flesh side out.   It never hung down over the edges of the stage floor, but was folded up neatly to make a kind of cushion.   The puncheon floor, at best never very smooth, was rather hard to sit upon; and letting a part of the skin hang down over the side would have been waste of good cushion material.

[4] In redrawing Goodbird's sketch this calf-skin has been omitted, that the construction of the stage floor might be shown.

The three poles on the right of the stage support another calf skin, used as a shield against the sun. The poles merely rested on the ground; they were not thrust into the soil. They could be shifted about with the sun, so that the watcher had shade in any part of the day.

The calf skin used for a sun shade hung on the poles head downward; whether it lay fur or flesh side down did not matter.

Skins dressed by Indians have holes cut along the edges for the wooden pins by which they are staked out on the ground to dry. The poles upholding the skin shade we cut of willows; and we were careful to trim off the branches, leaving little stubs sticking out on the trunk of the pole. These little stubs we slipped through some of the holes in the edge of the skin shade to uphold it and stay it in place. It was not necessary to bind the skin down with thongs; just slipping the stubs through the holes was enough.

Poles for a sun shade were cut indifferently of dry or green wood; and they lasted the entire season.

The ladder by which we mounted a watchers' stage rested against either of the corners next the tree, against one of the two beams supporting the floor; however we did not consider a watchers' stage to be sacred, and we placed the ladder anywhere it might be convenient.

The ladder was a cottonwood trunk, cut with three steps; more were not needed, as the stage floor was not high.

Sweet Grass's Sun Shade

If the tree sheltering a stage had scant foliage, we often cut thick, leafy cottonwood boughs and thrust them horizontally through the branches of the tree to increase its shade. It was a common thing for the watchers to tie a robe across the face of the tree for the same purpose.

If no tree grew in the garden, a small cottonwood with thick, leafy branches was cut and propped against the south or sunny side of the stage.

There was an old woman named Sweet Grass who had no tree in her garden. She built a stage just like that in Goodbird's sketch (figure 9). To shade it I remember she cut several small cottonwood trees and set them in holes made with her digging stick, along the south side of her stage. They stood there in a row and shaded the stage quite effectively. Her stage stood rather close to the edge of her garden.

The Watchers

The season for watching the fields began early in August when green corn began to come in; for this was the time when the ripening ears were apt to be stolen by horses, or birds, or boys. We did not watch the fields in the spring and early summer, to keep the crows from pulling up the newly sprouted grain; such damage we were content to repair by replanting.

Girls began to go on the watchers' stage to watch the corn and sing, when they were about ten or twelve years of age. They continued the custom even after they had grown up and married; and old women, working in the garden and stopping to rest, often went on the stage and sang.

Two girls usually watched and sang together. The village gardens were laid out close to one another; and a girl of one family would be joined by the girl of the family who owned the garden adjoining. Sometimes three, or even four, girls got on the stage and sang together; but never more than four. A drum was not used to accompany the singing.

The watchers sometimes rose and stood upon the stage as they looked to see if any boys or horses were in the field, stealing corn. Older girls and young married women, and even old women, often worked at porcupine embroidery as they watched. Very young girls did not embroider.

Boys of nine to eleven years of age were sometimes rather troublesome thieves. They were fond of stealing green ears to roast by a fire in the woods. Sometimes—not every day, however—we had to guard our corn alertly. A boy caught stealing was merely scolded. "You must not steal here again!" we would say to him. His parents were not asked to pay damage for the theft.

We went to the watchers' stage quite early in the day, before sunrise, or near it, and we came home at sunset.

The watching season continued until the corn was all gathered and harvested. My grandmother, Turtle, was a familiar figure in our family's field, in this season. I can remember her staying out in the field daily, picking out the ripening ears and braiding them in a string.

Booths

There were a good many booths in the gardens that lay west of the village. Usually a booth stood at one side of every field in which was a watchers' stage.

To make a booth, we cut diamond willows, stood them in the ground in a circle, and bending over the leafy tops, tied them together. A few leafy branches were interwoven into the top to increase the shade; but there was no further covering.

A booth had a floor diameter of nine or ten feet, and was as high as I can conveniently reach with my hands—six feet.

The girls who sang and watched the ripening corn cooked in these booths. I often did so when I was a young girl; for cooking at the booth was done by all the watchers, even young girls of ten or twelve years. I have often seen my grandmother, Turtle, also, in her booth very early in the morning, in the corn season.

Eating Customs

A meal was eaten sometimes just after sunrise, or a little later; but we never had regular meal hours in the field. We cooked and ate whenever we got hungry, or when visitors came; or we strayed over to other gardens and ate with our friends. If relatives came, the watchers often entertained them by giving them something to eat.

To cook the meal a fire was made in the booth. Meat had been brought out from the village, dried or fresh buffalo meat usually. Fresh meat was laid on the coals to broil; dried meat was thrust on the end of a stick that leaned over the coals; and when one side was well toasted it was turned over.

Fresh squashes we boiled in clay or iron pots; a good many brass or copper kettles also were in use when I was young. We were fond of squashes.

A common dish was green corn and beans. The corn was shelled off the cob and boiled with green beans that were shelled also; sometimes the beans were boiled in the pod.

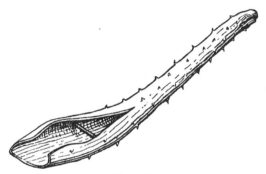

Figure 10
Redrawn from sketch by Goodbird of specimen made by
Buffalobird-woman.

To serve the corn and beans we poured the mess into a wooden bowl and ate with spoons made from the stems of squash leaves. Figure 10 is a sketch of such a spoon. The squash stem was split at one end and the split was held open by a little stick. Stems of leaves of our native squashes have tiny prickles on them, but these did not hurt the eater's lips. Leaf stems of native squashes I think are firmer and stronger than those of white men's squashes, such as we now raise.

My grandmother, Turtle, was a faithful watcher in our family field in the watching season. I remember she used to bring home in the evening all the uneaten corn she had boiled that day.

Youths' and Maidens' Customs

We always kept drinking water at the stage; and if relatives came out, we freely gave them to drink. But boys and young men who came were offered neither food nor drink, unless they were relatives.

Our tribe's custom in such things was well understood.

The youths of the village used to go about all the time seeking the girls; this indeed was almost all they did. Of course, when the girls were on the watchers' stage the boys were pretty sure to come around. Sometimes two youths came together, sometimes but one. If there were relatives at the watchers' stage the boys would stop and drink or eat; they did not try to talk to the girls, but would come around smiling and try to get the girls to smile back.

To illustrate our custom, if a boy came out to a watchers' stage, we girls that were sitting upon it did not say a word to him. It was our rule that we should work and should not say anything to him. So we sat, not looking at him, nor saying a word. He would smile and perhaps stop and get a drink of water.

Indeed, a girl that was not a youth's sweetheart, never talked to him. This rule was observed at all times. Even when a boy was a girl's sweetheart, or "love-boy" as we called him, if there were other persons around, she did not talk to him, unless these happened to be relatives.

Boys who came out to the watchers' stage, getting no encouragement from the girls there, soon went away.

A very young girl was not permitted to go to the watchers' stage unless an old woman went along to take care of her. In olden days, mothers watched their daughters very carefully.

Watchers' Songs

Most of the songs that were sung on the watchers' stage were love songs, but not all.

One that little girls were fond of singing—girls that is of about twelve years of age—was as follows:

> You bad boys, you are all alike!
> Your bow is like a bent basket hoop;
> You poor boys, you have to run on the prairie barefoot;
> Your arrows are fit for nothing but to shoot up into the sky!

This song was sung for the benefit of the boys who came to the near-by woods to hunt birds.

Here is another song; but that you may understand it I shall first have
to explain to you what ikupa' means.

A girl whom another girl loves as her own sister, we call her ikupa'.   I
think your word chum, as you explain it, has about the same meaning.
This is the song:

> "My ikupa', what do you wish to see?" you said to me.
> What I wish to see is the corn silk coming out on the growing ear;
> But what *you* wish to see is that naughty young man coming!

Here is a song that we sang to tease young men that were going by:

> You young man of the Dog society, you said to me,
> "When I go to the east on a war party, you will hear news of me how
>   brave I am!"
> I have heard news of you;
> When the fight was on, you ran and hid!
> And you think you are a brave young man!
> Behold you have joined the Dog society;
> Therefore, I call you just plain dog!

These songs from the watchers' stage we called mi'daxika, or gardeners'
songs.   The words of these I have just given you we called love-boy words;
and they were intended to tease.

There was another class of songs sung from the watchers' stage that did
not have love-boy words.   I will give you one of these, but to make it in-
telligible, I must first explain a custom of my tribe.

Clan Cousins' Custom

Let us suppose that a woman of the Tsi'stska Doxpa'ka marries a man
of the Midipa'di clan.   Their child will be a Tsi'stska; for we Hidatsas
reckon every child to belong to the clan of his mother; and the members
of the mother's clan will be clan sisters and clan brothers to her child.

Another woman of the tribe, of what clan does not matter, also marries
a Midipa'di husband; and they have a child.   The child of the first mother
and the child of the second we reckon as makutsati, or clan cousins, since
their fathers being of the same clan, are clan brothers.

In old times these clan cousins had a custom of teasing one another;
especially was this teasing common between young men and young women.
For example. a young man, unlucky in war, might be passing the gardens
and hear some mischievous girl, his clan cousin, singing a song taunting
him for his ill success.   From any one else this would be taken for the
deepest insult; but seeing that the singer was his clan cousin, the young
man only called out good humoredly, "Sing louder, cousin!"

I can best explain this custom by telling you a story.

Story of Snake-head-ornament

A long time ago, in one of our villages at Knife River, there lived a man Mapuksao'kihec, or Snake-head-ornament. He was a great medicine man; and in his earth lodge he kept a bull snake, whom he called "father."

When Snake-head-ornament started to go to a feast he would say to the bull snake, "Come, father, let us go and get something to eat!"

The snake would crawl up the man's body, coil about his neck and thrust his head forward over the man's crown and forehead; or he would coil about the man's head like the head cloth a hunter used to wear, with his head thrust forward as I have said.

Bearing the snake thus on his head, Snake-head-ornament would enter some man's lodge and sit down to eat. The snake however never ate with him, for his food was not the same as the man's; the bull snake's food was hide scrapings which the women of the lodge fed to him.

When Snake-head-ornament came home again he would say to the bull snake, "Father, get off."

The snake would creep down from the man's head, but before he entered his hole he would roll himself about on the earth lodge floor. Snake-head-ornament would say to him, "What are you doing? Do you think I am bad smelling, and do you want to wash off the smell from your body? It is you who are bad smelling; yet I do not despise *you!*"

The snake, hearing this, would creep into his hole as if ashamed.

Snake-head-ornament made up a war party and led it against enemies on the Yellowstone River. The party not only failed to kill any of the enemy, but lost three of their own men. This was a kind of disgrace to Snake-head-ornament; for as leader of the war party he was responsible for it. He thought his gods had deserted him; and when he came home he went about crying and mourning and calling upon his gods to give him another vision. He was a brave man and had many honor marks; and his ill success made his heart sore.

In old times, when one mourned, either man or woman, he cut off his hair, painted his body with white clay and went without moccasins; he also cut himself with some sharp instrument.

In those days also, when a man went out to seek his god, he went away from the village, alone, into the hills; and thus it happened that Snake-head-ornament, on his way to the hills, went mourning and crying past a garden where sat a woman, his clan cousin, on her watchers' stage. Seeing him, she began to sing a song to tease him:

> He said, "I am a young bird!"
> If a young bird, he should be in a nest;
> But he comes around here looking gray,
> And wanders aimlessly everywhere outside the village!

He said, "I am a young snake!"
If a young snake, he should stay in the hills among the red buttes;
But he comes around here looking gray and crying,
And wanders aimlessly everywhere!

When the woman sang, "he comes around here looking gray," she meant that the man was gray from the white clay paint on his body.

Snake-head-ornament heard her song, but knowing she was his clan cousin, cried out to her:

"My elder sister, sing louder! You are right; let my fathers hear what you say. I do not know whether they will feel shame or not; but the snake and the white eagle both called me 'son'!"

What he meant was that the snake and the white eagle were his dream gods; and that they had both called him "son," in a vision. In her song the woman had taunted him with this. If she had been any one but his clan cousin, he would have been beside himself with anger. As it was, he kept his good humor, and did her no hurt.

But the woman had sung her song for a cause. Years before, when Snake-head-ornament was quite a young man and as yet had won few honors he went on a war party and killed a Sioux woman. When he came home he was looked upon as a successful warrior; and he was, of course, proud that people now looked up to him. Not long after this, he joined the Black Mouth society. It happened, one day, that the women were erecting palisades around the village to defend it, and Snake-head-ornament, as a member of the Black Mouths, was one of those overseeing the work. This woman, his clan cousin, was rather slow at her task and did not move about very briskly. Snake-head-ornament, seeing this, approached her and fired off his gun close by her legs. She looked around, but seeing that it was Snake-head-ornament that had shot, and knowing he was her clan cousin, she did not get angry. Just the same she did not forget; and years after she had a good humored revenge in the taunting song I have given you.

Green Corn and Its Uses

The Ripening Ears

The first corn was ready to be eaten green early in the harvest moon, when the blossoms of the prairie golden rod are all in full, bright yellow; or about the end of the first week in August. We ate much green corn, boiling the fresh ears in a pot as white people do; but every Hidatsa family also put up dried green corn for winter. This took the place with us of the canned green corn we now buy at the trader's store.

I knew when the corn ears were ripe enough for boiling from these signs: The blossoms on the top of the stalk were turned brown, the silk on the end of the ear was dry, and the husks on the ear were of a dark green color.

I do not think the younger Indians on this reservation are as good agriculturists as we older members of my tribe were when we were young. I sometimes say to my son Goodbird: "You young folks, when you want green corn, open the husk to see if the grain is ripe enough, and thus expose it; but I just go out into the field and pluck the ear. When you open an ear and find it too green to pluck, you let it stand on the stalk; and birds then come and eat the exposed kernels, or little brown ants climb up the stalk and eat the ear and spoil it. I do not think you are very good gardeners in these days. In old times, when we went out to gather green ears, we did not have to open their faces to see if the grain was ripe enough to be plucked!"

Second Planting for Green Corn

Our green corn season lasted about ten days, when the grain, though not yet ripe, became too hard for boiling green.

To provide green corn to be eaten late in the season, we used to make a second planting of corn when June berries were ripe; and for this purpose we left a space, not very large, vacant in the field. In my father's family this second planting was of about twenty-eight hills of corn. It came ready to eat when the other corn was getting hard; but it often got caught by the frost. Nearly every garden owner made such a second planting; it was, indeed, a usual practice in the tribe.

Cooking Fresh Green Corn

Our usual way of cooking fresh, green corn, was to boil it in a kettle on the cob.

Fresh, green corn, shelled from the cob, was often put in a corn mortar and pounded; and then boiled without fats or meat. Prepared thus, it had a sweet taste and smell; much like that of the canned corn we buy of the traders.

Shelled green corn, in the whole grain, was also boiled fresh, mixed with beans and fats.

Roasting Ears

Green ears were sometimes roasted, usually by an individual member of the family who wanted a little change of diet. The women of my father's family never prepared a full meal of roasted ears that I remember; if any one wanted roasted, fresh, green corn, he prepared it himself.

When I wanted to roast green corn I made a fire of cottonwood and prepared a bed of coals. I laid the fresh ear on the coals with the husk removed. As the corn roasted, I rolled the ear gently to and fro over the coals. When properly cooked I removed the ear and laid on another.

.As the ear roasted, the green kernels would pop sometimes with quite a sharp sound.   If this popping noise was very loud, we would laugh and say to the one roasting the ear, "Ah, we see you have stolen that ear from some other family's garden!"

Green corn was regularly taken out of the garden to roast until frost came, when it lost its fragrance and fresh taste.   To restore its freshness, we would take the green corn silk of the same plucked ear and rub the silk well into the kernels of the ear as they stood in the cob.   This measurably restored the fresh taste and smell.

We did not do this if the ear was to be boiled, only if we intended to roast it.

For green corn, boiled and eaten fresh, we used all varieties except the gummy; for when green they tasted alike.   But for roasting ears we thought the two yellow varieties, hard and soft, were the best.

Mätu'a-la'kapa

A common dish made from green corn was mätu'a-la'kapa, from mätu'a, green corn; and la'kapa, mush, or something mushy; thus, wheat flour mixed with water to a thick paste we call la'kapa, even if unboiled.

Ripening green corn, with the grain still soft, was shelled off the cob with the tip of the thumb or with the thumb nail.   The shelled corn was pounded in a mortar and boiled with beans; it was flavored with spring salt.

Corn Bread

We also made a kind of corn bread from green corn.

Green ears were plucked and the corn shelled off with the thumb nail, so as not to break open the kernels.   Boiled green corn could be shelled with a mussel shell because boiling toughened the kernels; but unboiled green corn was shelled with the thumb nail.

Two or three women often worked at shelling the corn as it was rather tedious work.

When enough of the corn had been shelled, it was put in a corn mortar and pounded.

Some of the ears were naturally longer than others: a number of these had been selected and their husks removed.   Some of these husks were now laid down side by side, but overlapping like shingles, until a sheet was made about ten inches wide.

Another row of husks was laid over the first, transversely to them; and so until four or five layers of the green husks were made, each lying transversely to the layer of husks beneath.

The shelled corn, pounded almost to a pulp, was poured out on this husk sheet, and patted down with the hand to a loaf about seven or eight inches square, and an inch or two thick. However, this varied; a girl would make a much smaller loaf than would a woman preparing a mess for her family.

The ends of the uppermost layer of husks were now folded over the top of the loaf, leaf by leaf; then the next layer of husks beneath; and so until the ends of all the husks were folded over the top of the loaf, quite hiding it.

Two or three husk leaves had been split into strips half an inch to three quarters of an inch in width. These strips were tied together to make bands to bind the loaf. Three bands passed around the loaf each way, or six bands in all.

No grease nor fat, nor any seasoning, had been added to the loaf; the pounded green corn pulp was all that entered into it.

The loaf made, now came the baking. The ashes in the fire place in an earth lodge lay quite deep. A cavity was dug into these ashes about as deep as my hand is long. Into the bottom of this cavity live coals and hot ashes were raked, and upon these the loaf was laid; a few ashes were raked over the top, and upon these ashes live coals were heaped. The loaf baked in about two hours.

We called this loaf naktsi', or buried-in-ashes-and-baked. Soft white and soft yellow corn were good varieties from which to make this buried-and-baked corn, as we called it.

Drying Green Corn for Winter

Every Hidatsa family put up a store of dried green corn for winter. This is the way in which I prepared my family's store.

In the proper season I went out into our garden and broke off the ears that I found, that were of a dark green outside. Sometimes I even broke open the husks to see if the ear was just right; but this was seldom, as I could tell very well by the color and other signs I have described. I went all over the garden, plucking the dark green ears, and putting them in a pile in some convenient spot on the cultivated ground. If I was close enough I tossed each ear upon the pile as I plucked it; but as I drew further away, I gathered the ears into my basket and bore them to the pile.

I left off plucking when the pile contained five basketfuls if I was working alone. If two of us were working we plucked about ten basketfuls.

Green corn for drying was always plucked in the evening, just before sunset; and the newly plucked ears were let lie in the pile all night, in the open air. The corn was not brought home on the evening of the plucking, because if kept in the earth lodge over night it would not taste so fresh and sweet, we thought.

The next morning before breakfast, I went out to the field and fetched the corn to our lodge in the village. As I brought the baskets into the lodge,

I emptied them in a pile at the place marked *B* in figure 11, near the fire.

Sitting at *A*, I now began husking, breaking off the husks from each ear in three strokes, thus: With my hand I drew back half the husk; second, I drew back the other half; third, I broke the husk from the cob. The husks I put in a pile, *E*, to one side. No husking pegs were used, such as you describe to me; I could husk quite rapidly with my bare hands.

As the ears were stripped, they were laid in a pile upon some of the discarded husks, spread for that purpose. The freshly husked ears made a pretty sight; some of them were big, fine ones, and all had plump, shiny kernels. A twelve-row ear we thought a big one; a few very big ears had fourteen rows of kernels; smaller ears had not more than eight rows.

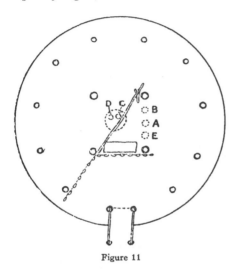

Figure 11

Two kettles, meanwhile, had been prepared. One marked *D* in figure 11, was set upon coals in the fireplace; the other, *C*, was suspended over the fire by a chain attached to the drying pole. The kettles held water, which was now brought to a boil.

When enough corn was husked to fill one of these kettles, I gathered up the ears and dropped them in the boiling water. I watched the corn carefully, and when it was about half cooked, I lifted the ears out with a mountain sheep horn spoon and laid them on a pile of husks.

When all the corn was cooked, I loaded the ears in my basket and bore them out upon the drying stage, where I laid them in rows, side by side, upon the stage floor. There I left them to dry over night.

The work of bringing in the five basketfuls of corn from the field and boiling the ears took all day, until evening.

In the morning the corn was brought into the lodge again. A skin tent cover had been spread on the floor and the half boiled ears were laid on it, in a pile. I now sat on the floor, as an Indian woman sits, with ankles to the right, and with the edge of the tent cover drawn over my knees, I took an ear of the half boiled corn in my left hand, holding it with the greater end toward me. I had a small, pointed stick; and this I ran, point forward, down between two rows of kernels, thus loosening the grains. The right hand row of the two rows of loosened kernels I now shelled off with my right thumb. I then shelled off all the other rows of kernels, one row at a time, working toward the left, and rolling the cob over toward the right as I did so.

There was another way of shelling half boiled corn. As before, I would run a sharpened stick down two rows of kernels, loosening the grains; and I would then shell them off with smart, quick strokes of a mussel shell held in my right hand. We still shell half boiled corn in this way, using large spoons instead of shells. There were very few metal spoons in use in my tribe when I was a girl; mussel shells were used instead for most purposes.

If while I was shelling the corn, a girl or woman came into the lodge to visit, she would sit down and lend a hand while we chatted; thus the shelling was soon done.

The shelling finished, I took an old tent cover and spread it on the floor of the drying stage outside. On this cover I spread the shelled corn to dry, carrying it up on the stage in my basket.

At night I covered the drying corn with old tent skins to protect it from dampness.

The corn dried in about four days.

When the corn was well dried, I winnowed it. This I sometimes did on the floor of the drying stage, sometimes on the ground.

Having chosen a day when a slight wind was blowing, I filled a wooden bowl from the dried corn that lay heaped on the tent cover; and holding the bowl aloft I let the grain pour slowly from it, that any chaff might be winnowed out.

The corn was now ready to be put in sacks for winter.

Corn thus prepared we called maada′ckihĕ, from ada′ckihĕ, treated-by-fire-but-not-cooked, a word also used to designate food that has been prepared by smoking.

All varieties of corn could be prepared in this way.[5]

The Arikaras on this reservation have a different way of preparing and drying green corn. They make a big heap of dried willows, and upon these lay the ears, green and freshly plucked, in the husk. When all is ready, they set fire to the willows, thus roasting the corn; and they often roast a great pile of corn at one time, in this way. The roasted ears are husked and shelled, and the grain dried, for storing. Corn that has been roasted in the Arikara way, dries much more quickly than that prepared by boiling.

Of late years some Mandan and Hidatsa families occasionally roast their corn in imitation of the Arikara way; but I never saw this done in my youth.

I do not like to eat food made of this dried, roasted corn; it is dirty!

[5] "My wife is drying half-boiled corn on the ear this year. This way we find makes the dried corn sweeter, but takes longer to dry it. We cook it in winter by dropping the ear, cob and all, into the pot. This method of drying corn was known also in old times."—EDWARD GOODBIRD

Mapë'di (Corn Smut)

Mapë'di

Mapë'di is a black mass that grows in the husk of an ear of corn; it is what you say white men call corn smut fungus. Sometimes an ear of corn appears very plump, or somewhat swelled; and when the husk is opened, there is no corn inside, only mapë'di, or smut; or sometimes part of the ear will be found with a little grain at one end, and mapë'di at the other. These masses of mapë'di, or corn smut, that we found growing on the ear, we gathered and dried for food.

There is another mapë'di that grows on the stalk of the corn. It is not good to eat, and was not gathered up at the harvest time. The mapë'di that grows on the stalk is commonly found at a place where the stalk, by some accident, has been half broken.

We looked upon the mapë'di that grew on the corn ear as a kind of corn, because it was borne on the cob; it was found on the ears the grain of which was growing solid, or was about ready to be eaten as green corn. We did not find many mapë'di masses in one garden.

Harvest and Uses

We gathered the black masses and half boiled and dried them, still on the cob. When well dried, they were broken off the cob. These broken off pieces we mixed with the dried half boiled green corn, and stored in the same sack with them.

Mapë'di was cooked by boiling with the half-boiled dried corn. We did not eat mapë'di fresh from the garden, nor did we cook it separately. Mapë'di, boiled with corn, tasted good, not sweet, and not sour.

I still follow the custom of my tribe and gather mapë'di each year at the corn harvest.

The Ripe Corn Harvest

Husking

As the corn in the fields began to show signs of ripening, the people of Like-a-fishhook village went hunting to get meat for the husking feasts. This meat was usually dried; but if a kill was made late in the season, the meat was sometimes brought in fresh.

When the corn was fully ripened, the owners of a garden went out with baskets, plucked the ears from the stalks and piled them in a heap ready for the husking. The empty stalks were left standing in the field.

A small family sometimes took as many as three days to gather and husk their ripe corn; this was because there were not many persons in the family to do the work.

In a big family, like my father's, harvesting was more speedily done. We had a large garden, but we never spent more than one day gathering up the corn, which we piled in a heap in the middle of the field.

The next day after the corn was plucked, we gave a husking feast. We took out into the field a great deal of dried meat that my mothers had already cooked in the lodge; or we took the dried meat into the field and boiled it in a kettle near the corn pile. We also boiled corn on a fire near by. The meat and corn were for the feast.

Instead of dried meat, a family sometimes took out a side of fresh buffalo meat and roasted it over a fire, near the corn pile.

Having then arrived at the field, and started a fire for the feast, all of our family who had come out to work sat down and began to husk. Word had been sent beforehand that we were going to give a husking feast, and the invited helpers soon appeared. There was no particular time set for their coming, but we expected them in one of the morning hours.[6]

For the most part these were young men from nineteen to thirty years of age, but a few old men would probably be in the company; and these were welcomed and given a share of the feast.

There might be twenty-five or thirty of the young men. They were paid for their labor with the meat given them to eat; and each carried a sharp stick on which he skewered the meat he could not eat, to take home.[7]

The husking season was looked upon as a time of jollity; and youths and maidens dressed and decked themselves for the occasion.

---

[6] Buffalobird-woman means that the huskers arrived in the fields in the morning to begin the day's labors. More than one corn pile might be husked in a single day. — GILBERT L. WILSON

[7] Water Chief having strolled into the cabin while Buffalobird-woman was dictating, here interrupted with the following:

"The owner of a field would come and notify the crier of some society, as the Fox or Dog society, or some other. The crier would go on the roof of the society's lodge and call, 'All you of the Fox society come hither; they want you to husk. When you all get here, we will go to that one's garden and husk the corn!'

"We young men of the society all gathered together and marched to the field to which we were bidden. In old times we took our guns with us, for the Sioux might come up to attack us. As we approached the field we began to sing, that the girls might hear us. We knew that our sweethearts would take notice of our singing. The girls themselves did not sing.

"At the corn pile in each garden would be the woman owner and maybe two or three girls. On our way to some field, if we passed through other fields with corn piles at which were girls, each young man looked to see if his sweetheart was there; and if he saw her he would yell, expecting that she would recognize his voice.

"Sometimes two societies husked at one corn pile. Any of the societies might be asked. If the pile was too big for one society, another society was asked, if the owner could afford the food for the feast.

"Different societies would be husking in different gardens all at the same time.

"Sometimes a group of young men belonging to different societies were asked to come and husk. This was chiefly at small gardens; the societies were usually asked to come and husk the big corn piles of the larger gardens.

"If a society went early, they got through just after midday. By early I mean nine o'clock in the morning.

"When we had finished husking one pile, we went to another. We worked late, by moonlight, even.

"Some man of the family and his wife would be out all night and watch by the corn if they had not gotten all the husked ears borne in to the village. Also while the pile awaited husking watchers stayed by to protect against horses."

Of course each young man gave particular help to the garden of his sweetheart. Some girls were more popular than others. The young men were apt to vie with one another at the husking pile of an attractive girl.

Some of the young men rode ponies, and when her corn pile had been husked, a youth would sometimes lend his pony to his sweetheart for her to carry home her corn. She loaded the pony with loose ears in bags, bound on either side of the saddle, or with strings of braided corn laid upon the pony's back.

The husking season, like the green corn season, lasted about ten days. The young men helped faithfully each day, and when they had husked all the corn in one field, they moved to another. Thus all the corn piles were speedily husked.

The husking was always done in the field. We never carried the corn to the village to be husked, as the husks would then have dried, and hurt the hands of the husker. As we plucked the ears, we piled them in a heap in the field, to keep the husks moist and soft.[8]

Rejecting Green Ears

As the huskers worked they were careful not to add any green ears to the husked pile. A green ear would turn black and spoil, and be fit for nothing.

Every husker knew this; and if a young man was helping another family husk, he laid in a little pile beside him, any green ears that he found. These green ears belonged to him, to eat or to feed to his pony.

Last year a white man hired me to gather the corn in his field and husk it; and I kept all the green ears for myself, for that is my custom. I do not know whether that white man liked it or not. It may be he thought I was stealing that green corn; but I was following the custom that I learned of my tribe.

I am an Indian; if a white man hires me to do work for him, he must expect that I will follow Indian custom.

[8] "Corn in old times was gathered in September. A basket was carried on the back and the corn was tossed into it over the shoulder, or the basket was set on the ground and filled. This work was done by the women. The corn having been plucked, the owner of the field notified people what food she wanted to serve—meat or boiled corn-and-beans—and young men came to husk the corn. A pile might be three or four feet high and twenty feet long. The men huskers sat on one side of the pile and the women on the other. The big ears were strung in braids. A braid was long enough to reach from the thigh around under the foot and up again to the other side of the thigh. A husker would try the newly made braid with his foot as he held the ends in his hands. Unless this was done a weak place in the string might escape notice and the braid break, and all the others would then laugh.

"Small ears were tossed into one place. Four or five women would carry off these ears in baskets; they bore the filled baskets right up the ladder to the top of the drying stage. The braided strings were often borne home on the backs of ponies, ten strings on a pony. They were hung like dead snakes on the railings above the floor of the stage to dry.

"Boys and young men went to the husking bees because of the fun to be had; they wanted to see the girls!"—EDWARD GOODBIRD (related in 1909).

Braiding Corn

Most of the corn as it was husked was tossed into a pile, to be borne later to the village. This was true of all the smaller and less favored ears; the best of the larger ears were braided into strings.

As we husked, if a long ear of good size and appearance was found, it was laid aside for braiding. For this purpose the husk was bent back upon the stub of the stalk on the big end of the ear, leaving the three thin leaves that cling next to the kernels still lying on the ear in their natural position. The part of the husk that was bent back was cut off with a knife; the three thin leaves that remained were now bent back on the ear, and the ear was laid aside. Another ear was treated in the same way and laid beside the first, also with its thin leaves bent back. And thus, until a row of ears lay extended side by side upon the ground, all the ears lying point forward.

Another row was started; and the ears, also lying point forward and leaned against the first row, were laid so as to cover the thin bent-back leaves of the first row, to protect them from the sun. As the braiding was done with these thin leaves, if they were too dry—as the sun was very apt to make them—they would break.

When a quantity of these ears, all with thin husk leaves bent back, had accumulated, one of the huskers passed them to someone of the young men, who braided them; or one of the women of the family owning the field might braid them.

Even with care the thin leaves were sometimes too dry for the braider to handle safely; and he would fill his mouth with water and blow it over the leaves.

Fifty-four or fifty-five ears were commonly braided to a string; but the number varied more or less. In my father's family, we often braided strings of fifty-six or fifty-seven ears.

I do not know why this number was chosen; but I think this number of ears was about of a weight that a woman could well carry and put upon the drying stage.

When the string was all braided, the braider took either end in his hand, and placing his right foot against the middle of the string, gave the ends a smart pull. This stretched and tightened the string, and made it look neater and more finished; it also tried if there might be any weak places in it.

We braided all varieties of corn but two, atą'ki tso'ki, or hard white, and tsi'di tso'ki, or hard yellow. These varieties we reckoned too hard to parch, and for this reason they were not braided. We did, however, sometimes parch hard yellow to be pounded up into meal for corn balls.

The strings of braided corn were borne to the village on the backs of ponies. Some families laid ten strings on a pony; but in my father's family we never laid on so many, believing it made too heavy a load for the poor beast.

The braided strings were hung to dry on the drying stage upon the railing that lay in the upper forks; and if there was need, poles or drying rods were laid across the rails and strings were hung over these also.[9]

These drying rods were laid across only where the forks supported the rails (at the same places the staying thongs were tied), for at these places the stage could better bear the weight of the heavy strings of corn; the drying rods were bound at either end to the railing, to stay them.

The Smaller Ears

Meanwhile the smaller and less favored ears were being carried home in baskets. It took the members of my father's family a whole day, and the next day following until late in the afternoon, to get this work done.

Each carrier, as she brought in a basket of corn, ascended the log ladder of the stage and emptied the corn on the stage floor. Here the corn lay in a long heap, in the middle of the floor; for a free path was always left around the edge for us women; having this path for our use, we did not have to tread on the corn as we moved about. Also, if a pony came in with a load of braided corn, the heavy strings could be handed up to us women on the stage as we moved around in this free path.

As I now remember, our family's husked corn when piled on the stage floor, made a heap about eight yards long and four yards wide, and about four feet high in the middle, from which point the pile sloped down on all sides. This was the loose corn, the smaller ears; and besides these there were about one hundred strings of braided corn hung on the railing above the heap. I give these measurements, judging as nearly as I can from the size of our drying stage, and from our average yearly corn yield, when I was a young woman. I think the figures are approximately accurate.

For about eight days the corn lay thus in a long heap upon the stage. At the end of that time the ears on the top of the heap had become dry and smooth and threatened to roll down the sides of the pile. We now took drying rods and laid them along the floor against the posts, two or three of them, for the whole length of the stage on either side, and on the ends of the stage. Planks split from cottonwood trunks were leaned against these drying rods, on the side next the corn. The corn heap was now spread evenly over the floor of the drying stage for the depth of about

[9] "Sometimes for fun we lads used to take long poles with nooses on the end and snare off one ear of a braid of corn as it hung drying; for the braids were soft when fresh. An ear broken off, we would run off and make a fire and parch the corn. This was when we were little fellows, ten or eleven years old. The owner would run after us, and if he caught one of us, whipped him. However, this was our custom; and the owner and the boy's father both looked upon it as a kind of lark, and not anything very serious."
—EDWARD GOODBIRD

a foot; the split planks prevented the dry smooth ears from sliding off the stage. The dry ears had a tendency to roll or slide down the sides of the corn pile, as fresh ears did not.

This spreading out the corn heap evenly had also the effect of stirring up the underlying ears and exposing them to the air.

If rain fell while the corn was thus drying on the stage, it gave us no concern. The corn soon dried again, and no harm was done it.

The corn, spread thus in an even heap, took about three more days to dry, or eleven days in all. Then we began threshing.

Drying the Braided Ears

The strings of braided corn hanging on the rails at the top of the posts of the drying stage, dried much more quickly than the loose ears heaped on the stage floor. The wind, rattling the dry ears of the strings together, was apt to shell out the drying kernels; it was therefore usual for us before threshing time to tie these braids together so that the wind could not rattle them.

To do this I would ascend the ladder and make my way along the edge of the stage floor, making places in the corn with my feet as I walked, so that my feet would be on the stage floor and not tread on the drying corn. I would push ten of the braided strings together on the rail or the drying rod on which they hung, and tie them by passing around them a raw hide thong.

These braided strings, bound thus in bundles of ten, hung on the stage until we were ready to store them in the cache pit; and this we could not do until we had our main harvest, the loose ears, threshed and ready to store also.

Seed Corn

Selecting the Seed

I have said that for braiding corn we chose the longest and finest ears. In my father's family we used to braid about one hundred strings, some years less, some years more, as the season had been wet or dry; for the yield of fine ears was always less in a dry year. Of these braided strings we selected the very best in the spring for seed.

My mothers reckoned that we should need five braided strings of soft white, and about thirty ears of soft yellow, for seed. Of ma'ikadicakĕ, or gummy, we raised a little each year, not much; ten ears of this, for seed, my mothers thought were a plenty.

Hard white and hard yellow corn, I have said, were not braided, because not used for parching. For seed of these varieties, some good ears were taken from the drying pile on the corn stage and stored in the cache pit for the next year with loose grain of the same variety.   The ears were not put in a sack, but thrown in with the loose grain.

When I selected seed corn, I chose only good, full, plump ears; and I looked carefully to see if the kernels on any of the ears had black hearts. When that part of a kernel of corn which joins the cob is black or dark colored, we say it has a black heart.   This imperfection is caused by plucking the ear when too green.   A kernel with a black heart will not grow.

An ear of corn has always small grains toward the point of the cob, and large grains toward the butt of the ear.   When I came to plant corn, I used only the kernels in the center of the cob for seed, rejecting both the small and the large grains of the two ends.

Seed corn was shelled from the cob with the thumb; we never threshed it with sticks.   Sometimes we shelled an ear by rubbing it against another ear.

Keeping Two Years' Seed

Corn kept for seed would be best to plant the next spring; and it would be fertile, and good to plant, the second spring after harvesting.   The third year the seed was not so good; and it did not come up very well. The fourth year the seed would be dead and useless.

Knowing that seed corn kept good for at least two years, it was my family's custom to gather enough seed for at least two years, in seasons in which our crops were good.   Some years, in spite of careful hoeing, our crops were poor; the ears were small, there was not much grain on them, and what grain they bore was of poor quality.   We did not like to save seed out of such a crop.   Also, frost occasionally destroyed our crop, or most of it.

When, therefore, we had a year of good crops, we put away seed enough to last for two years; then, if the next year yielded a poor crop, we still had good seed to plant the third season.

In my father's family we always observed this custom of putting away seed for two years; and we did this not only of our corn, but of our squash seeds, beans, sunflower seeds, and even of our tobacco seeds; for if I remember rightly, the tobacco fields were sometimes injured by frost just as were our corn fields.

Not all families in our village were equally wise.   Some were quite improvident, and were not at all careful to save seed from their crops. Such families, in the spring, had to buy their seed from families that were more provident.

Saving a good store of seed was therefore profitable in a way.   In my father's family we often sold a good deal of seed in the spring to families that wanted.   The price was one tanned buffalo skin for one string of braided seed corn.

Like-a-fishhook village being dismantled, July 1887; the drying stage in the foreground is floored in Arikara fashion, with a mat of willows, and it holds what looks like a pile of squashes (photographed by George Curtis; American Museum of Natural History 15979)

Owl Woman with an antler rake, 1914 (photographed by Gilbert Wilson; Minnesota Historical Society 42348)

Owl Woman showing how to use a digging stick, 1914 (photographed by Gilbert Wilson; Minnesota Historical Society 42342)

Sioux Woman, Goodbird's wife, hoeing squash to demonstrate the use of a bone hoe, 1912 (photographed by Gilbert Wilson; Minnesota Historical Society 9448-A)

Owl Woman gathering sunflowers in a skin basket, 1914 (photographed by Gilbert Wilson; Minnesota Historical Society 42218)

Scarecrow a in corn field, 1918 (photographed by Gilbert Wilson; Minnesota Historical Society 41284)

Husking corn, 1909; the woman braids the best ears (photographed by Gilbert Wilson; Minnesota Historical Society 9627-A)

Drying loose and braided ears of corn on a corn stage, 1909 (photographed by Gilbert Wilson; American Museum of Natural History 286444)

Owl Woman pounding corn into meal in a corn mortar, 1914 (photographed by Gilbert Wilson; Minnesota Historical Society 42324)

Owl Woman slicing squash with a bone squash knife, 1916 (photographed by Gilbert Wilson; Minnesota Historical Society 42264)

Goodbird sitting under slices of drying squash, strung on spits and laid on a structure built to resemble a corn stage (photographed by Gilbert Wilson; Minnesota Historical Society 42094)

Woman winnowing beans, 1909 (photographed by Gilbert Wilson; Minnesota Historical Society 9635-A)

Model of a cache pit, 1912; made by Buffalo Bird Woman in the bank of the Missouri River to show cross section (photographed by Gilbert Wilson; Minnesota Historical Society 9446-A)

Even to-day, families on this reservation come to me to buy seed corn and seed beans. A handful of beans, enough for one planting, I sell for one calico—enough calico, that is, to make an Indian woman a dress, or about ten yards.

THRESHING CORN

The Booth

The threshing season was always a busy one, for all the families of the village would be threshing their corn at the same time.

Corn was threshed in a booth, under the drying stage.

To make the booth, I began with the section at one end of the stage. As is shown in figure 12, on the posts *A* and *D*, and *B* and *C*, were bound

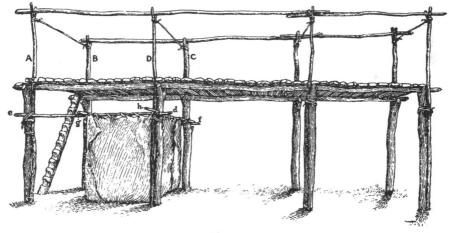

Figure 12

The figure has been redrawn from sketches by Goodbird. The original is a stage now standing on the reservation, but with mat of willows for floor; to this Goodbird added a threshing booth as he saw used by his grandmother when he was a boy. Goodbird's sketches are closely followed, excepting that the floor of slabs is restored. The figure tallies in every respect with Buffalobird-woman's description, and the model made by her for the American Museum of Natural History.

two poles, *e* and *f*, at about two feet below the stage floor; upon these were bound two other poles, *g* and *h*; the poles *e*, *f*, and *h* were bound outside of the posts that supported them.

A long raw hide thong was used for the corner ties. The first pole was raised in position and bound firmly to the post; and if a second pole was to be laid over the first—as was done at two of the corners—the thong was drawn up and made to bind it also to the post. We always kept a number of these raw hide thongs in the lodge against just such uses as this; they were strong, and served every purpose of ropes; we oiled them to keep them soft.

A tent cover was now fetched out of the lodge. Tents were of different sizes, from those of seven, to those of sixteen buffalo cow hides. A woman used whatever sized tent cover she owned; but a cover of thirteen skins was of convenient size.

Figure 13

Around the curved bottom of the tent cover was a row of holes, through which wooden pins were driven to peg the tent to the ground. The tent cover was bound to the four over-hanging poles, inside of the four posts, by means of a long thong woven in and out through the holes, as shown in figure 13.

Bound thus to the poles, and quite enclosing the space within them, the tent cover made a kind of booth. The upper parts of the cover, in-

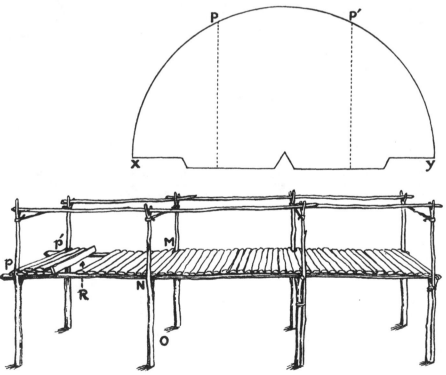

Figure 14

cluding the smoke flaps, that now hung sweeping the ground, were drawn in and spread flat on the ground to make a floor for the booth; and stones laid upon them weighted the cover against the wing.

In figure 12 the four posts, *A*, *B*, *C*, and *D*, enclose one section of the drying stage; the booth did not enclose the whole ground space of this section, but about three fifths of it.

Figure 14, I think, will explain the arrangement of the booth. The end corners, *X* and *Y*, were bound to opposite posts, *M* and *N*, respectively, the lapping edges, at *O*, forming a door through which the threshers entered the booth; *P* and *P'* were bound to posts at *p* and *p'*; the final corner, *M*, was left untied until the threshers had entered and were ready to begin their task. (Compare with figure 12, in which, however, the posts are differently lettered.)

Before they did this they went above and removed the planks and drying rods laid around the edge of the stage floor, and pushed the corn back toward the middle of the floor into a long heap again, that it might not fall over the edge, now that the planks were taken away. One of the floor planks was now removed, at *R*. Through the aperture thus made, corn was pushed down to left and right of *R*; this was continued until there was a pile of corn just under the aperture, and running the width of the booth, about eighteen or twenty inches high.

The threshers now entered the booth and tied the corner at *M*, closing the door. In my father's family there were usually three threshers, women; and they sat in a row on the floor

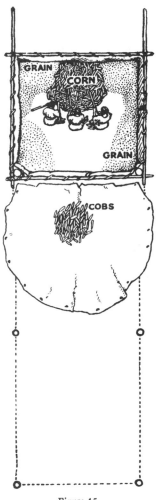

Figure 15

of the booth, facing the pile of corn. Each woman had a stick for a flail, with which she beat the corn.

Flails were of ash or cottonwood. An ash flail would be about three and a half feet long and from three quarters of an inch to an inch in diameter, and was cut green. A cottonwood flail was seldom used green; and as it was therefore lighter than the green ash, a cottonwood flail was a little greater in diameter, but of the same length. We were careful that a flail should not be too heavy, lest it break the kernels in the threshing. Kinikinik sticks were sometimes used for flails.

A diagram (figure 15) has been drawn to illustrate how I worked in a threshing booth when I was a young woman. As shown, I sat on the extreme left; one of my mothers and my sister sat as indicated, on my right. More than three seldom worked in a threshing booth at the same time, at least in our family; however, I have known my sister, Not-frost, to make a fourth. I have even known five to be threshing in the booth of some other family in the village, but never more than five.

To thresh the corn, I raised my flail and brought it down smartly, but not severely, upon the pile of corn. The grain as it was thus beaten off the dry cobs would fall by its own weight into the pile, and work its way to the bottom; while the lighter cobs would come to the top of the pile.

Beating the ears with the flails caused many of the kernels to leap and fly about; but the tent cover, enclosing the booth, caught all these flying kernels. It was, indeed, for this that the booth was built.

As the cobs, beaten empty of grain, accumulated on the pile, we drew them off and cast them out of the door of the booth upon a tent cover, spread to receive them, under the middle section of the stage. Many of these cobs had a few small grains clinging to them; and these must be saved, for we wasted nothing.

Having paused then to throw out the cobs, we returned to the pile and thrust our flails in under it, drawing them upward through the corn, thus working the unthreshed ears to the top. As much as we could, we tried to keep the unthreshed ears in the middle of the pile, and the threshed grain pushed to right and left, as will be seen by studying the diagram. To thresh one pile, or filling of corn in a booth, took a half day's work.

Order of the Day's Work

Our habit was to begin quite early in the morning, enclose the booth with the tent cover, and set to work threshing; finishing the first filling, or pile, about midday. In the afternoon we began a second pile, first heaping the already threshed grain to right and left, and behind the threshers.

I have said that on the ground under the second section of the stage, a second tent cover was spread to catch the cobs. A part of this tent cover was drawn in under the edge of the booth to help carpet the floor of the booth.

At the end of the day we turned our attention to the pile of cobs; and with our thumbs we shelled off every grain that clung to the cobs. From the cobs of a day's threshing we collected about as many grains of corn as would fill a white man's hat. This was taken into the booth and thrown on the pile of threshed grain.

We now disposed of the grain for the night. If we had gotten through threshing rather early in the day, we bore the newly threshed grain in baskets into the lodge, and emptied it into a bull boat.

If we had gotten through our threshing rather late in the day, we made the door of the booth tight, and left the grain on the booth floor throughout the night.

The Cobs

The day's threshing over, we attended to the cobs. I have said that we shelled off any kernels that clung to them after threshing, so that they were now quite clean of grain.

All day long, as we threshed, we had watched that no horses got at the cobs to trample and nibble them, or that any dog ran over them, or any children played in them. Then, in the evening, if the weather was fine, and there was little wind, one of my mothers or I carried the cobs outside of the village to a grassy place and heaped them in a pile about five feet high. A pile of cobs of such a height I usually gathered from a day's threshing.

In our prairie country, on a fair day, the wind usually dies down about sunset; and now, when the air was still, I fired the cob pile. As the pile began to burn, I could usually see the burning cob piles of two or three other families lighting up the gathering dusk.

I had to stay and watch the fire, to keep any mischievous boys from coming to play in the burning heap. Children of from ten to fifteen years of age were quite a pest at cob-firing time. They had a kind of game they were fond of playing. Each would cut a long, flexible, green stick, and at the edge of the Missouri he would get a ball of wet mud and stick it on his stick. He would try to approach one of the burning piles, and with his stick, slap the mud ball smartly into the burning coals, some of which, still glowing, would stick in the wet mud. Using the stick as a sling, the child would throw the mud ball into the air, aiming often at another child. Other children would be throwing mud balls at one another at the same time, and these, with the bits of glowing charcoal clinging to them, would go sailing through the air like shooting stars. Knowing very well that the children would get into my burning cobs if I even turned my back, I was careful to stay by to watch.

At last the fire had burned down and the coals were dead; and nothing was left but a pile of ashes. It was now night, and I would go home. Early the next morning, before the prairie winds had arisen, I would go out again to my ash heap. On the top of the ashes, if nothing had disturbed them in the night and an unexpected wind had not blown them about, I would find a thin crust had formed. This crust I carefully broke and gathered up with my fingers, squeezing the pieces in my hand into little lumps, or balls. Sometimes I was able to gather four or five of these little balls from one pile of ashes; but never more than five.

These balls I carried home. There were always several baskets hanging in the lodge, ready for any use we might want of them; and it was our habit to keep some dried buffalo heart skins, or some dried buffalo paunch skins, in the lodge, for wrappers, much as white families keep wrapping paper in the house. The ash balls I wrapped up in one of these skins, into a package, being careful not to break the balls. I put the package in one of the baskets, to hang up until there was occasion for its use.

These ash balls were used for seasoning. I have explained elsewhere how we used spring salt to season our boiled corn; and that every day in the lodge, we ate mä′dạkạpa, or pounded dried ripe corn boiled with beans. But in the fall, instead of seasoning this dish with spring salt, or alkali salt as you call it, we preferred to use this seasoning of ash crust.

In my father's family, for each meal of mä′dạkạpa we filled the corn mortar three times, two-and-a-half double handfuls of corn making one filling of the mortar. Each time we filled the mortar, we dropped in with the corn a little of the ash crust, a bit about as big as a white child's marble. Finally, a piece about as big, or perhaps a little larger, was also dropped into the boiling pot.

We Indians were fond of this seasoning; and we liked it much better than we did our spring salt. We did not use spring salt, indeed, if we had ash balls in the lodge.

We called these ash balls mä′dạkạpa isĕ′pĕ, or mä′dạkạpa darkener.

We did not make ash balls if the dogs or horses had trampled on the cobs; or if children had mussed in the fire; nor would we make ash balls if the day had not been rather calm, for a high wind was sure to blow dust into the cobs.

We burned cobs and collected ash balls after every threshing day, unless hindered by storm or high wind. But even if the harvest was a good one, the ash balls that we got from the burned cobs for seasoning never lasted long. We were so fond of seasoning our food with them that every family had used up its store before the autumn had passed.

Winnowing

I have said that after the day's threshing we stored the newly threshed grain for the night, either in the booth or in a bull boat in the earth lodge; and that we then fired the cobs that had accumulated during the day.

The next morning we spread an old tent cover outside the lodge, near the drying stage; and we fetched the loose grain of the previous day's threshing out of the booth, or the earth lodge and spread it evenly and thinly upon the tent cover. The grain was here left to dry until evening.

A little before sunset, and before the prairie wind had died down, we fetched baskets and winnowed the grain. The basket was half filled with grain, held aloft, and the grain poured gently out in the wind. Wooden bowls were often used for winnowing, instead of baskets; but they did not hold as much grain.

The winnowing over, I would take up a few grains of the corn to test with my teeth. If, when I bit a kernel in two, it broke with a sharp, snappy sound, I knew it was quite dried; if it broke dull and soft, I knew the grain needed another day's drying; but at the most, this second day's drying was enough.

The winnowed grain, now well dried, was borne into the earth lodge and stored temporarily in bull boats. In the diagram (figure 16), is shown where the bull boats full of grain used

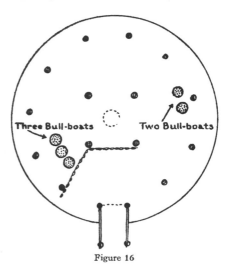

Figure 16

to stand in my father's lodge. Some years our harvest filled three bull boats of threshed grain; some years it filled five. In the year illustrated by this diagram, there were three bull boats standing between the planks at the left of the door, and the fire; and two bull boats on the other side of the fire, all full of grain.

The threshed grain, I have said, received its final drying and winnowing upon a tent cover (or covers) spread on the ground near the earth lodge. It was my own habit always to spread these tent covers beside the drying stage on the side farthest away from the lodge. However, the particular spot where the winnowing was done, was determined by the convenience of the household.

We did not usually thresh consecutive days. We threshed one day; dried the grain and winnowed it the second; and threshed again the third day.

Removing the Booth

During these days the booth did not remain always in one place. When the corn on the floor of the first section had all been threshed, the booth was removed to another section. I will now explain how this was done.

In figure 17 my son has diagramed the floor plan of my mothers' stage and threshing booth, as I remember them.

The stage stands in front of Small Ankle's lodge, which faces toward the west. The stage is divided into three sections, *A*, *B*, *C*. The posts upon which the floor of the stage rests are *d, e, f, g, h, i, j, k*.

The booth was first raised under section *A*, based upon *fg*, and enclosing ground space *lmfg*.

Sometimes we got up early, bound the poles to the posts and erected our booth before breakfast; then after we had eaten, three or four of us would go out to thresh, one first going up to push down the corn. She raised a plank along the side, *fg*, just within the booth; this, if the door of

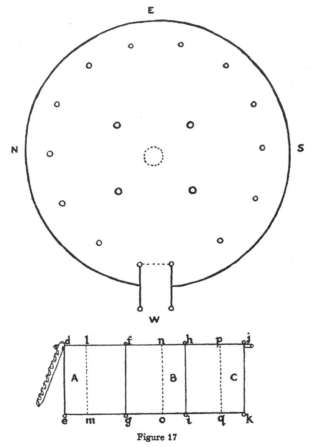

Figure 17

Ground plan of earth lodge here accompanies that of stage to show relative positions of the two structures. The stage always stood, as here, directly before the lodge entrance. The figures are drawn to scale.

the booth was on the side *lm*. The corn on the floor of the stage in section *A* was then shoved down as wanted.

The corn pushed down for one threshing, made a pile running the width of the booth, and about forty inches wide and twenty inches high. When the pile was threshed one of the women went up and shoved down another pile. The corn in one section was threshed in about three such piles.

Sometimes, if we worked hard and had plenty of help, we threshed one whole section in one day; but the beating, beating, beating of the corn was hard work, and we more often stopped when wearied and rested until the next day. I have already said that we often spent the next day at the lighter work of drying and winnowing.

When the corn in section *A* was all threshed, the booth was moved over under the floor of section *B*, enclosing *fgno*; and again a plank was taken up to let down the corn. Now this plank was always taken up above the side of the booth opposite the door; and the door was always placed down wind. Thus, if the wind was from the north, the door would be placed on the south side of the booth, and the plank was taken up on the north side, just within the booth. Corn was always threshed in the booth on the side opposite the door.

Sections *A* and *B* of my mothers' stage, as shown in diagram (figure 17) contained only yellow corn. Section *C*, or a part of it, contained white corn. Braided strings of corn were also hung all around the railing above, but these were not to be threshed.

Section *B* having been threshed, the booth was removed to section *C*, enclosing *hiqp*. I have said that this section had white corn. Now this white corn was piled toward the south end of the stage; and between it and the yellow corn was left a narrow vacant place on the floor. Above this vacant place, meat was often dried; but this meat was removed when we were ready to thresh.

Placing the booth to enclose *hiqp*, directly under the vacant place, made it easy for us to raise a plank here to push down the white corn. If we had placed the booth on the south end of this section, we should have had to dig into the corn piled here, in order to raise a plank.

Our family's threshing lasted about five days in a year of good yield; if the year was a poor one, threshing lasted only two or three days.

Threshing Braided Corn

The strings of braided corn were stored in the cache pit (which I will describe later) in the whole ear. If, during the winter, or the following spring, I wanted to thresh a string of braided corn, I put the whole string into a skin sack; and this sack I beat and shook, turning it over and around until all the grain had fallen off the cobs. The sack was then emptied.

Amount of Harvest

Our harvested corn, in a good year, lasted my father's family until the next harvest, with a small quantity even then unused. Some years we ran out of corn before the harvest came, but not often.   We ate our corn as long as it lasted, not husbanding it toward the last, because we knew there were elk and buffalo and antelope to be had for the hunting.   If we ran out of corn at all, it was about the first of August; sometimes a little earlier.   Sometimes when we had eaten all our last year's harvest there was a small quantity from the previous season's harvest with which we eked out our shortage.

My mothers, however, were industrious women, and our shortage, if any, was never for long.   Some families, not very provident, had consumed all their harvest as early as in the spring; but such never happened in my father's family.

Sioux Purchasing Corn

The Standing Rock Sioux used to buy corn of us, coming up in mid-summer, or autumn.   They came not because they were in need of food, but because they liked to eat our corn, and had always meat and skins to trade to us.   For one string of braided corn they gave us one tanned buffalo robe.

VARIETIES OF CORN

Description of Varieties

We raised nine well marked varieties of corn in our village.   Following are the names of the varieties:

Atą'ki tso'ki (White hard)	Hard white
Atą'ki (White)	Soft white
Tsï'di tso'ki (Yellow hard)	Hard yellow
Tsï'di tapa' (Yellow soft)	Soft yellow
Ma'ikadicakĕ (Gummy)	Gummy
Do'ohi (Blue)	Blue
Hi'ci cĕ'pi (Red dark)	Dark red
Hi'tsiica (Light-red)	Light red
Atą'ki aku' hi'tsiica (White, kind of light red)	Pink top

Our Hidatsa word for corn is ko'xati; but in speaking of any variety of corn, the work ko'xati is commonly omitted. In like manner, atą'ki means white; but if one went into a lodge and asked for "atą'ki" it was always understood to mean soft white corn.

Of the nine varieties, the atą'ki, or soft white, was the kind most raised in our village. The ma'ïkadicakĕ, or gummy, was least raised, as almost its only use was in making corn balls.

In my father's family, we raised two kinds of corn, tsï'di tso'ki, or hard yellow; and atą'ki, or soft white.

The names of the varieties suggest pretty well their characteristics. The atą'ki aku' hi'tsiica, or white-with-light-red, was marked by a light red or pink color toward the top or beard end of the ear. The name pink-top which you suggest for this variety will, I think, do for an English name, if the literal translation of the Indian term is, as you say, rather clumsy.

We planted each variety of corn separately. We Indians understood perfectly the need of keeping the strains pure, for the different varieties had not all the same uses with us.

How Corn Travels

We Indians knew that corn can travel, as we say; thus, if the seed planted in one field is of white corn, and that in an adjoining field is of some variety of yellow corn, the white will travel to the yellow corn field, and the yellow to the white corn field.

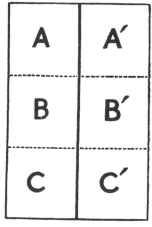

Figure 18

Perhaps you do not understand what I mean by corn traveling. Well, let us suppose that there are two fields lying side by side, the one in yellow, the other in white corn. When the corn of the two fields is ripe, and the ears are opened, it will be found that many of the ears in the yellow rows that stand nearest the white field will have white kernels standing in the cob; also, in the rows of white corn that stand nearest the yellow field, there will be many ears with yellow kernels mixed in with the white kernels.

We Indians did not know what power it was that causes this. We only knew that it was so. We also knew that when a field stands alone, away from other fields, and is planted with white corn, it will grow up in white corn only; there will not be any yellow grains in the ears. And so of any other variety.

Sometimes two women, owning adjoining fields, would make an agreement; they would divide their fields into sections and plant the corresponding sections on opposite sides of the division line alike. Thus in the diagram (figure 18), A and A' may be planted in a variety of yellow corn; B and B' may be planted in beans and squashes; and C and C' may be planted in a variety of white corn; but even this did not make so very much difference; still the corn traveled.

We thought that perhaps the reason of this was that the ground here was soft, or mellowed and broken by cultivation. We thought corn could not travel readily over hard, or unbroken ground; and as you notice in the diagram, although the two patches of yellow corn are separated from the white corn by the two patches of squashes and beans, yet the beans and squashes are in soft, or cultivated ground. We thought corn traveled more easily over soft ground.

However, we really did not know what made corn travel; we just knew that it did.

USES OF THE VARIETIES

Atą'ki Tso'ki

I think that perhaps at first, there was but one variety of corn, atą'ki tso'ki, or hard white; and that all other varieties have sprung from it. I know that when we plant hard white seed, ears often develop that show color in the grain. Sometimes ears are produced bearing pink grains toward the beard end of the cob; such ears we call i'puta (top) hi'tsiiea (pink); that is, pink top, or light-red top. In color these ears differed in no wise from atą'ki aku' hi'tsiica.

Hard white was very generally raised, nearly every family in the tribe having a field of it.

There were two chief dishes chiefly prepared from hard white corn; these I will now describe.

Māpi' Nakapa'. I put water in a pot, and in this I dropped a section of a string of dried squash, with some beans. Dried squash was always strung on long grass strings; and having, from one of these strings. cut off a piece I tied the ends together, making a wreath, or ring, four or five inches in diameter. It was this ring of dried squash slices that I dropped into the pot. When well boiled, I lifted the squash slices out by the string and dropped them into a wooden bowl, where I mashed them and chopped them fine with a horn spoon. The mashed squash I dropped back into the kettle again, with the beans; the now empty string I threw away.

Meanwhile corn had been parched, and some buffalo fats had been held over the coals on a stick, to roast. The parched corn and roast fats I pounded together in the corn mortar; and the pounded mass I stirred into the kettle. The mess was now ready to be eaten.

This dish we called mäpi'-nakapa', or pounded-meal mush; from mäpi,' something pounded, and nakapa', mush, something mushy.

The dish was especially a morning meal; after eating it we started to work.

Mä'nakapa. A second way of preparing hard white corn was as follows: I pounded the corn in a mortar to a meal, but without first parching it. Most of this meal was fine, but there were many coarser bits in it, some of them as big as quarter grains of corn.

Water was put in a kettle; I added the pounded meal, and when it boiled put in beans. No fats were added.

As the mess boiled. I stirred it with a wooden paddle to prevent scorching; I did not stir with a horn spoon as the hot water softened and spoiled the horn.

When well boiled, the mess was served.

We called this dish mä'nakapa'.[10]

A seasoning of spring salt, as we called it, was often added. A small palmful of the salt was mixed with a little water in a horn spoon; this

---

[10] In 1910 Buffalobird-woman gave an interesting and detailed account of the making of a clay pot. A newly made pot, she explained, was rubbed over with boiled pounded-corn meal; and she added this rather humorous variation of the recipe above:

"This mush, or boiled, pounded-corn meal was made thus:

"A clay pot was three-quarters filled with water and put on the fire to boil. Meanwhile, twelve double handfuls of corn were pounded in the corn mortar; usually we pounded three or four double handfuls at a time. This began after breakfast; it was work and made us women sweat. The corn was hard, ripe corn, yellow or white.

"These twelve double handfuls were thrown into the pot of now boiling water, and boiled for half an hour. As there was no grease in the pot, we had to stir the contents with a smooth stick to keep from sticking.

"As the corn boiled a scummy substance would rise to the top. To this the woman cooking would touch the point of her horn spoon, and carry it to her tongue and lick it off. When she could taste that it was sticky enough, she knew that it was time to add beans. It took, as I have said, about half an hour for the corn to boil to this point.

"She now added some spring salt. This is alkaline salt which we gathered about the mouth of springs. It was white. The woman put some of this salt in a cup and made a strong liquor—in old times instead of a cup she used a horn spoon. She now added the salt liquor to the mess. It took about enough of this white salt to make a heaping tablespoonful to one pot of this corn mess. As the salt liquor was poured into the pot, the woman held her hand over the mouth of the cup, so that if any pieces of grass or other refuse were in it, they would be strained out by her fingers.

"The corn when it is pounded does not pound evenly; and so when it was put into the pot, the finer part of the meal was cooked first. This rose to the top, and in old times was skimmed off. The coarser parts of the meal took longer to cook; but the skimmed-off part, when the other was done, was poured back into the pot again.

"When the pounded corn meal had now all cooked and the salt had been added, the beans were put in— red, spotted, black, or shield-figured, we did not have white beans in very old times; they were brought in by white men. The pot was now let boil until the beans were done. Beans were always added to the pot.

"A pot of corn meal and beans was [almost] always on the fire in the lodge. The boys of the lodge liked to come around when the corn was cooking and dip horn spoons into the thick, rising liquor, and lick it off as I have described the woman doing as she cooked.

"It was this sticky, rising liquor taken off the boiling corn to keep and return to it, that was used to rub over a newly made pot. When this was done, the pot was ready to boil corn in.

"After using a pot, it was usually rubbed over with the residue of the boiled corn meal, or mush, because this made the pot look better and last longer.

"The skimmed-off liquor from a pot of boiling corn meal was also fed to a baby whose mother had died, and whose family could not hire a woman to nurse it."

dissolved the salt and let the sand and dirt drop to the bottom. The dissolved salt was poured off through the fingers, held to the mouth of the horn spoon; this strained out the sand and dirt. The salt turned the mush slightly yellow.

As the soft mush boiled up in the cooking, we were fond of dipping a horn spoon into it, and licking off the back of the spoon. This was especially a children's habit.

Also at morning and evening meals we ate hard white corn parched and mixed with fats; or madapo'zi i'ti'a, boiled whole corn.

Atą'ki

This is a soft, or as you call it, a flour corn, and was perhaps the favorite variety grown by us. The word atą'ki means white; but when applied to corn we translate soft white, to distinguish from atą'ki tso'ki, or hard white.

The use of atą'ki, or soft white, was very general, since it could be made into almost every kind of corn food used by us. "It is the one variety," we used to say, "that can be used in any and every way."

Soft white corn, parched and pounded into a meal, was boiled with squash and beans to make mäpi' nakapa'. The unparched grain was pounded for meal to make mä'nakapa; but although good, we did not think the mush made from soft white meal was as good as that from the hard white corn meal.

Boiled Corn Ball. A less frequent dish made from soft white corn was boiled corn balls; it was made only from the dried ripe grain.

I pounded a quantity of grain into meal, and poured the meal into a pot having hot water—but not too much water—stirring it well about. I now lifted out some of the mass into my left palm and patted it down with my right, making a cake about as big around as a baking powder biscuit, but not so thick. This cake I dropped into a pot of boiling water, where it sank to the bottom. I continued until the pot was full, or until I had all I wished to cook.

No salt or other seasoning was added.

As the pot boiled, one could see the corn cakes move around in the water; but they never floated, nor did they break apart. The boiling lasted about an hour.

In olden days we ate these corn balls alone; now we more often eat them with coffee.

Tsĭ'di Tso'ki and Tsĭ'di Tapä'

The two varieties of tsĭ'di, or golden yellow corn, could be pounded and boiled to make mush, or mä'dakapa; or they could be boiled whole, to make mądąpo'zi i'ti'a.

Mạdạpo'zi I'ti'a. For this dish I put the shelled ripe grain, with fats, in a pot and boiled them until I saw the kernels break open; then I added beans, and when these were boiled, the mess was served. This dish we called mạdạpo'zi i'ti'a. I do not know the derivation of mạdạpo'zi; i'ti'a means large. I think you can translate "corn boiled whole."

Hard yellow and soft yellow corn, roasted in the green ear, tasted sweet, as if a little sugar were in them. Especially was this true at the time when kernels were beginning to turn yellow. At this time each kernel shows a little yellow spot on the very top. For this reason this season was called tsi'dotsxĕ, or yellow-drop time; for the little yellow spot looked like a drop on the top of the kernel.

Other Soft Varieties

Do'ohi, or blue, hi'ci cĕ'pi, dark red, and hi'tsiica, light red, were all soft corns and were cooked and prepared and stored just like ata'ki; these four varieties tasted exactly alike, if cooked in the same way.

Ma'ikadicakĕ

Ma'ikadicakĕ, or gummy corn, is of different colors; some is of a light red; some yellow flaked with red; and some is in color like hard white; but all these slightly differing strains are alike in this, that when the kernels dry they shrink up and become rough, or wrinkled. The name, ma'ikadicakĕ, comes from kadi'cakĕ, or gum-like.

Ma'ikadicakĕ was the least grown of our five principal varieties of corn; however, a good deal of this variety is still raised on this reservation.

Ma'ikadicakĕ was sometimes roasted green, when the kernels chewed up gummy in the mouth; but the one recognized use of this variety was to make corn balls.

Mä'pĭ Mĕĕ'pĭ I''kiuta, or *Corn Balls.* Into a clay pot while yet cold, I put shelled corn and set it on the fire. As the grain parched, I stirred it with a stick. The heat made the kernels pop open somewhat, but not much.

Meanwhile fats were roasted over the coals on the point of a stick; and these and the parched grain were dropped into the corn mortar and pounded together. I then reached into the mortar and took out a handful of the meal, which being oily with the fats, held together in a lump. This lump I squeezed in my fingers and then tapped it gently on the edge of the mortar, making a slight dent or groove, lengthwise, in one side of the lump. The lump or ball—it was not exactly round—I dropped into a wooden bowl. The process was repeated until the bowl was full.

Our native name for corn ball is mä'pi mĕĕ'pĭ i''kiuta, from mä'pi, something pounded, mĕĕ'pĭ, mortar, and i''kiuta, hit or pressed against;

that is pounded meal pressed against the mortar; but we translate, just corn ball.

Corn balls were an acceptable present for a woman to give her daughter to take to her husband; the son-in-law might himself eat the corn balls, or share them with his parents or sisters.

As I have said, the one recognized use of gummy corn was for parching to make corn balls; but any of the soft corns could be used to make corn balls, as soft yellow, soft white, blue, light red, and the like.

Parched Soft Corn. Corn of any of the soft varieties parched in a pot as just described, was often carried by hunters or travelers to be eaten as a lunch. The corn was carried in a little bag made by drying a buffalo's heart skin.

Parching Whole Ripe Ears. We parched the whole ears, sometimes, of ripe soft white and soft yellow corn. We had many squash spits piled up in the rear of the lodge behind the beds; these made excellent roasting sticks. The ear was stuck on the end of the stick and held over the coals.

Parching ripe corn on the ear was a winter custom; but boys herding horses in the summer also parched whole ears sometimes for their midday lunch.

We did parch other kinds of corn thus, besides soft white and soft yellow, but they were not so good.

The gummy was not cooked in this way.

Parching Hard Yellow Corn with Sand. We sometimes parched hard yellow corn in a clay pot of our own make, with sand. Down on the sand bars by the Missouri we found clean, pure sand; if I wanted to parch hard yellow, I put a handful of this sand in my clay pot.

The pot I now set on the coals of the fire place until the sand within was red hot. With a piece of old tent skin to protect my hand, I drew the pot a little way from the coals and dropped a double handful of corn within. I stirred the corn back and forth over the sand with a little stick.

When I thought the corn was quite heated through, I put the pot back on the coals again, still stirring the corn with the stick. Very soon all the kernels cracked open with a sharp crackling noise; they burst open much as you say white man's popcorn does.

Hard yellow corn parched in this way was softer than even the soft corns parched in a pot without sand.

No variety of corn was good cooked in this way, except hard yellow; no other kind would do.

Mᶐdᶐpo'zi Pᶐ'kici, or Lye-Made Hominy. There was another way in which we prepared hard and soft yellow and hard and soft white; this was to make it into hominy with lye.

I collected about a quart of ashes; only two kinds were used, cottonwood or elm wood ashes. When I was cooking with such wood and thought of making hominy, I was careful to collect the ashes, raking away the other kinds first.

I put on an iron kettle nearly full of water, and brought it to a boil. Into the boiling water I put the ashes, stirring them about with a stick. Then I set the pot off to steep for a short time.

When the ashes had settled I poured the lye off into a vessel and cleaned the pot thoroughly.

In earlier times the ashes were boiled in an earthen pot as indeed I have often seen it done when I was a girl. I was not quite twenty when we bought an iron pot for cooking. Before that we used only earthen pots for cooking in our family.

Having cleaned the pot I poured the lye back into it, put the pot on the fire, and added shelled, ripe, dried corn. This I boiled until the hulls came off the grain and the corn kernels appeared white.

I added a little water, and took the pot off the fire; I drained off the lye.

I poured water into the pot and washed the corn, rubbing the kernels between my palms; I drained off the water.

I poured in water and washed the corn a second time, in the same way; I drained off the water.

Again I put water in the pot and boiled the corn in it. As the corn was already soft, this boiling did not take long. I now added fats, and beans, and sometimes dried squash, all at the same time; and the pot I replaced on the fire. When the beans and squash were cooked, the mess was ready to eat.

Corn so prepared we call mądąpo'zi pą'kici, or boiled-whole-corn rubbed. It is so called because the hulls of the kernels were rubbed off between the palms at the time the corn was washed in water after the lye was poured off.

General Characteristics of the Varieties

We Hidatsas thought that our five principal varieties of corn, hard and soft white, hard and soft yellow, and gummy, had characteristics that marked them quite distinctly one from the other.

For one thing, they had each a distinct taste. If at night I were given to eat of hard white corn, or hard yellow or soft yellow, I could at once tell each from any of the others. If I were given mush at night made from these three varieties, each by itself, I could distinguish each variety, not by its smell, but in my mouth by taste.

Meal made by pounding ripe hard white corn became thick and mushy when boiled in a pot.

Tsï'di tapa', or soft yellow corn, was quite soft to pound when we made meal of it; and the boiled meal, or mush, seemed to contain a good deal of water in it—that is, it seemed thin and gruel-like when we came to eat it.

To pound tsï'di tso'ki, or hard yellow corn, into meal took a long time; but when it had been pounded and the meal boiled into food, it was very good to eat and had an appetizing smell.

Of the nine varieties I have named, the atạ'ki, or soft white, was the earliest maturing. If seeds of all nine varieties were planted at the same time, the soft white would always be the first to ripen in the fall; and the tsï'di tso'ki, or hard yellow, would be the last to ripen.

Although the blue, light red, dark red, pink top, and soft white were all soft or flour corns, yet the soft white was the earliest to ripen. I reckon the soft white, also, to be the softest of all our varieties of corn.

I also rate the hard yellow and hard white as equal in value. Both are equally hard, and can not be pounded up into the fine flour or meal which we get from the soft varieties.

The hard yellow and soft yellow we thought were the best varieties from which to prepare half-boiled dried corn for winter storing. The

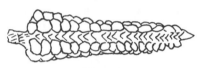

Figure 19

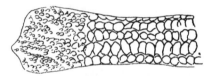

Figure 20

dark and light reds were also used, and if not quite so good, were but little inferior. Indeed, for half-boiled dried corn, all varieties were used, even the ma'ikadicakĕ, or gummy; but this last we did not think a good variety for this way of putting up corn. Our gummy corn had but one well recognized use; it was good for parching to make corn balls.

Fodder Yield

I do not think there was any perceptible difference in the fodder yield of the various races of corn which we Hidatsas cultivated; but the fodder yield was always much heavier in rainy years. In a dry season, the stalks of the corn would be small and weak; and the leaves would be smaller than in seasons of good rainfall.

Developing New Varieties

We Hidatsas knew that slightly differing varieties could be produced by planting seeds that varied somewhat from the main stock. A woman named Good Squash used to raise a variety of corn that tasted just like soft white. This corn had large swelling kernels with deep yellow, almost reddish, stripes running down the sides of the grain. We called it Adaka'-

dahu-ita ko'xati, or Arikaras' corn, though it was not Arikara corn at all. Good Squash's daughter, Hunts Water, lives on this reservation; she may have some of the seed of this variety.

Sport Ears

Names and Description

Quite often ears of corn appear that are marked by some unusual form; and for the more marked of these forms, we had special names. Following are some of them:

Na''ta-tawo'xi. From na''ta, grain; and tawo'xi, a name applied to youth, or the young, and conveying the idea of small. This is an ear of corn having seventeen or eighteen rows of very small kernels. Our largest ears of corn had usually but fourteen rows of kernels of normal size.

In the old legends of my tribe appear many women bearing this name Na''ta-tawo'xi.

Wi'da-Aka'ta. From wi'da, goose; and aka'ta, roof of the mouth. This is an ear having two rows of corn on either side, with vacant spaces on the cob between the double rows; often, toward the larger end of the ear, the two rows will expand into three. Goodbird has made a drawing of such an ear (figure 19). A wi'da-aka'ta ear, we thought, looks like the roof of the mouth of a goose.

I'ta-Ca'ca. Forked face, or cloven face; from i'ta, face. A kind of double ear. Goodbird has made a drawing of one (figure 20).

Okĕi'jpita. From o'kĕ, or o'ki, head-ornament, plume; i'jpu, top; and i'ta, fruit. This is a small ear that sometimes appears at the top, on the tassel of the plant.

Okĕi'jpita ears, if large enough, we gathered and put in with the rest of the harvest; but smaller ears of this kind, hardly worth threshing, we gathered and fed to our horses. Sometimes, if the harvesters were in haste, these ears were left in the field on the stalk; a pony was then led into the field to crop the ears.

I'tica'kupadi. I'tica'kupadi, or muffled head; so called because the kernels come down and cover the face or bearded end of the cob quite to the point. We thought such an ear looked like a man with his head muffled up in his robe.

Muffled-head ears were more numerous in good crop years than in poor years; and we thought such ears, if otherwise well favored, made good seed corn.

CHAPTER V

SQUASHES

PLANTING SQUASHES

Sprouting the Seed

Squash seed was planted early in June; or the latter part of May and the first of June.

In preparation for planting, we first sprouted the seed.

I cut out a piece of tanned buffalo robe about two and a half feet long and eighteen inches wide, and spread it on the floor of the lodge, fur side up.

I took red-grass leaves, wetted them, and spread them out flat, matted together in a thin layer on the fur. Then I opened my bag of squash seeds, and having set a bowl of water beside me, I wet the seeds in the water— not soaking them, just wetting—and put them on the matted grass leaves until I had a little pile heaped up, in quantity about two double-handfuls.

I next took broad leaved sage, the kind we use in a sweat lodge, and buck brush leaves, and mixed them together. At squash planting time, the sage is about four inches high

Into the mass of mixed sage-and-buck-brush leaves, I worked the wetted squash seeds, until they were distributed well through it. The mass I then laid on the grass matting, which I folded over and around it. Finally I folded the buffalo skin over that, making a package about fifteen by eighteen inches. We called this package kaku'i kida'kci, squash-thing-bound, or squash bundle.

This squash bundle I hung on the drying pole near one of the posts. The bundle did not hang directly over the fire, but a little to one side. Sed si femina in domo menstrua erat, she should tell it so that the package of seeds could be removed to the next lodge, or they would spoil.

After two days I took the bundle down and opened it. From a horn spoon I sipped a little tepid water into my mouth and blew it over the seeds. I took care that the water was neither too hot nor too cold, lest it kill the seeds. I rebound the bundle and hung it up again on the drying pole. At the end of another day the seeds were sprouted nearly an inch and were ready to plant.

I took a handful of the grass-and-leaves, and from them separated the sprouted squash seeds. A wooden bowl had been placed beside me with a little moist earth in it. Into this bowl I put the seeds, sprinkling a little earth over them to keep them moist. I was now ready to begin planting.

68

Planting the Sprouted Seed

Usually two or three women did the family planting, working together. One woman went ahead and with her hoe loosened up the ground for a space of about fifteen inches in diameter, for the hill. Care was taken that each hill was made in the place where there had been a hill the year before. I am sure that in olden times we raised much better crops, because we were careful to do so; using the same hill thus, each year, made the soil here soft and loose, so that the plants thrived.

One woman, then, as I have said, with her hoe, loosened up the soil where an old hill had stood, and made a new hill, about fifteen inches in diameter at the base. Following her came another woman who planted the sprouted seeds.

Four seeds were planted in each hill, in two pairs. The pairs should be about twelve inches apart, and the two seeds in each pair, a half inch apart. The seeds were planted rather under, or on one side of the hill, and about two inches deep in the soil. A careful woman planted the seeds with the sprouts upright; but even if she did not do this, the sprouts grew quickly and soon appeared through the soil.

We had a reason for planting the squash seeds in the side of the hill. The squash sprouts were soft, tender. If we planted them in level ground the rains would beat down the soil, and it would pack hard and get somewhat crusted, so that the sprouts could not break through; but if we planted the sprouts on the side of the hill, the water from the rains would flow over them and keep the soil soft. Likewise, we did not plant the sprouted seeds on the top of the hill because here too the rain was apt to beat the soil down hard.

We Indian women helped one another a good deal in squash planting; especially would we do turns with our relatives. If I got behind with my planting, some of my relatives, or friends from another family, would come and help me. When a group of relatives thus labored together, four women commonly went ahead making the hills, and two women followed, planting the sprouted seeds.

Harvesting the Squashes

The squash harvest began a little before green corn came in. It was our custom to pick squashes every fourth morning; and the fourth picking— twelve days after the first picking—brought us to green corn time.

The first picking was, naturally, not very large—three or four basketfuls, I think, in my father's family; and these we ate ourselves. The basket used for bringing in the squashes was about fifteen inches across the mouth and eleven inches deep.

The second picking was about ten basketfuls, enough for us to eat and spare a little surplus to our neighbors. After this each picking increased until a maximum was reached, and then the pickings decreased in size. The fifth or sixth picking was usually the largest.

The pickings were made before sunrise. In my father's family, one of my mothers and I usually attended to the actual picking. It was her habit to get up early in the morning, go to the field and pluck the squashes from the vines, piling them up in one place in the garden. She returned then to the lodge; and after the morning meal, the rest of us women of the household went out and fetched the squashes home in our baskets.

Squashes grow fast, and unless we picked them every four days, we did not think them so good for food. Moreover, squashes that were four days old we could slice for drying, knowing that the slices would be firm enough to retain their shape unbroken. If the squashes were plucked greener, the slices broke, or crumbled.

We could tell when a squash was four days old. Its diameter then was about three and a quarter inches; some a little more, some a little less; but we chiefly judged by the color of the fruit. A white squash should just have rid itself of green; a green colored squash should have its color a dark green. We could judge quite accurately thus, by the state of the colors.

The hills yielded some three, some two, some only one squash at a picking. I have made as many as six trips to our family garden for the squashes of a single picking; our garden was distant as far as from here to Packs Wolf's cabin—three quarters of a mile.

We picked a good many squashes in a season. One year my mother fetched in seventy baskets from our field. I have known families to bring in as many as eighty, or even a hundred baskets, in a season.

The baskets, as they were brought in, were borne up on the drying stage, and the squashes emptied out on the floor for slicing and drying; squashes not cooked and eaten fresh were sliced and dried for winter, excepting those saved for seed.

Slicing the Squashes

Slicing squashes for drying began about the third picking. Sometimes, in good years, a few squashes might be sliced at the second picking; but at the third picking, slicing and drying began in earnest.

When the squashes, emptied from the baskets, made a great heap on the floor of the drying stage, the women of the family made a feast, cooking much food for the purpose; some old women were then invited to come and cut up the squashes with knives, into slices to dry. We regarded these old women as hired; and I remember that in my father's family we hired sometimes eight, sometimes ten, sometimes only six. I think that at the time I was a young woman, when my mothers made such a feast, about ten old women came.

These old women ascended the drying stage, and sat, five on either side of the pile of squashes. Each of the old women had a squash knife in her hand, made of the thin part of the shoulder bone of a buffalo, if it was an old-fashioned one; butcher knives of steel are now used.

The squashes were cut thus:

An old woman would draw a robe up over her lap, as she sat Indian fashion, with ankles to the right, on the floor of the stage. She took a squash in her left hand, and with her bone knife in her right, she sliced the squash into slices about three eighths of an inch thick.

The squash was sliced from side to side, not from stem to blossom. An old woman slicing squash would take up a squash, cut out the stem pit and the blossom, then turn the squash sidewise and slice, beginning on the side nearest her. The cut was made by pressing the bone blade downward into the squash as the latter lay in her palm.

The first three slices and the last three of a large squash; or the first two and the last two of a smaller squash, the old woman put beside her in a pile, as her earnings for her work; upon this pile also went any squash thought too small to be worth slicing.

These end slices we thought less valuable than those from the middle of the squash; and unlike the latter, they were not spitted on willow sticks, but were taken home by the old woman worker in her blanket, or her robe, or in something else in which she could carry them. About three sacks of these inferior slices would be carried home at one time by an old woman worker.

These less valuable slices being cut close to the rind were of solid flesh. The better slices had each a hollow in the center, caused by the seed cavity. The old women did not spit their solid slices on willows, but dried them on the ground, carefully guarding them against rain; for if wet, the drying slices would spoil.

Squash Spits

All the better slices, the ones to be retained by the family that hired the old women workers, were spitted on willow rods to dry.

These rods we called kaku'iptsa; from kaku'i, squash; and i'ptsa, spit, stringer. The word may be translated squash spit.

Squash spits were usually made of the small willows that we call mi'da hatsihi'ci, or red willow; from mi'da, wood; and hi'ci, light red. When the outer skin of one's finger, for example, is peeled off, the color of the flesh beneath we call hi'ci. This red willow however is not kinikinik, which white men call red willow.

A squash spit should be about half an inch in diameter; and its length should be measured from the center of my chest to the end of my index finger, as I do now; or about two feet, six, or two feet, seven inches.

A spit was sharpened at one end to a point. At the other end there was left about an inch of the natural bark like a button, to keep the squash slices from slipping off. The rest of the rod was peeled bare.

Small Ankle used to make our drying spits for us. He cut the rods in June or early July when the bark peeled off easily; he peeled off the bark with his teeth.

It was his habit to cut quite a number of rods at a time and after peeling them, he would tie them up in a bundle of about three hundred rods, so that they would dry straight—would not warp, I mean, in drying.

In seasons when they were not in use our squash spits were made into a bundle as big as I could hold in my two arms and bound about with two thongs. The bundle was stored away on the floor of the lodge, under the eaves, or in the atu'ti, as we called the space under the descending roof. The next year, in harvest time, the bundle was unbound and the spits examined to see if any had warped. Such warped ones were thrown away, and new ones were made to take their places.

Spitting the Slices

Each of the old women hired to slice our squashes worked with a pile of these squash spits beside her; and as she sliced a squash she laid aside those slices which she retained as her pay; and taking the others up in her right hand, she spitted them with a single thrust, upon one of the willow spits. The spitted slices were then separated about a half inch apart, so that the first two fingers of the hand could be thrust astraddle the spit between each slice and its neighbor. This was to give the slices air to dry.

One willow spit held the slices of four squashes, and two slices from a fifth squash, if the squashes were of average size.

Sometimes an old woman brought her granddaughter along to help her, the little girl spitting the slices as her grandmother cut them.

Drying rods, which I have already described, were laid across the upper rails of the stage; and each spit as it was loaded was laid with either end resting on a drying rod. The spits were laid with a certain method. Each projecting end bore two squash slices, which acted as a button to stay the spit from being blown down by the wind.

As the drying rods rested transversely on the upper rails, the spits which the rods bore lay parallel with the rails, and therefore lengthwise with the stage. The spits were laid with the heavier, or bark covered end toward the front, or ladder end of the stage, which in our family, was the right, as one came out of the lodge door.

When a pair of drying rods was quite filled with these loaded spits, they made what we called one i'tsaki—one walking stick, or one staff. We counted the quantity of squash we dried as so many staves.

We never laid the loaded spits on the floor of the stage, as the weight of the load caused the drying squash slices to warp, thus making them hard to handle.

In Case of Rain

If a sudden rain came up the day we began drying squash, we felt no concern, for the slices having just been cut, were still green and would not be harmed.

But if rain threatened the second day, or thereafter, we women ran up on the stage and drew the loaded spits toward the middle of the drying rods; and over them we spread hides, upon which we laid poles, or unused drying rods to weight the hides against the wind. Sometimes we even lashed the poles down with thongs.

If the drying squash got wet after the first day, the slices swelled up, and the fruit spoiled.

Drying and Storing

When the squash slices had dried for two days, two women of the family went up on the stage; and working, one from the front, the other from the rear end of the stage, they took the spits one by one, and with thumb and fingers of each hand slipped the drying slices into the middle of the spit, thus loosening them from it; and for the same purpose, the spit itself was turned and twisted around as it lay skewered through the slices. When well loosened, the squash slices were again spaced apart as before, and the spit was replaced on the rods, to be left for another day. On the evening of the third day the slices were dry enough to string.

The strings, three to six in number, had been prepared from dry grass. Each string was seven Indian fathoms long; we Hidatsas measure a fathom as the distance between a woman's two outstretched hands. Each grass string had a wooden needle about ten inches long, bound to one end.

All the slices on one spit were now slid off and the worker by a single thrust skewered the wooden needle through them and slid them down the long string to the farther end; this end of the string was now looped back and tied just above the first three or four slices of the dried squash that fell down the string; doing thus made these slices act as a button or anchor to prevent the rest of the squash slices from slipping off the string.

In stringing the squash slices, the spit was held in the right hand, the left hand straddling the spit with the index and second fingers. The slices were slid down the spit toward the right hand, the spit being then drawn out and cast away. The squash slices were held firmly in the first two fingers and thumb of the left hand and the needle was run through the hole left by withdrawing the spit.   As the spit had a greater diameter than the grass string, the slices easily slid down the string.

Figure 21

When stringing slices of squash myself, I always sat on the floor of the drying stage with a pile of loaded spits at my left side.   As I unloaded a spit, I dropped it at my right side.   The grass string hung over the edge of the stage floor, on the side nearest the lodge.   On the ground below I had spread some scraped hides, so that the squash slices, falling down the string, would not touch the ground and become soiled.

When a string became full, I tossed the end over the edge of the floor, letting it fall down upon the heap on the scraped hides.

The needle used to skewer the slices was bound to the end of the grass string two inches or more from its extremity, as shown in figure 21.   When the string was filled, one had but to turn the needle athwart, and it became a button or anchor, preventing the slices from slipping off.

The strings filled with dried squash slices, were now taken into the lodge.   Between the right front main post of the lodge and the circle of outer posts and near the puncheon fire screen at the place it bent in toward the wall, a stage had been built.   Two forked posts, about as high as my head, supported a pole ten or twelve feet long; and over this pole the strings of squash were looped, care being taken that they hung at a height to let the dogs run under without touching and contaminating the squash.   I speak of the right front main post; I use right and left in the Indian sense, which assumes that an earth lodge faces the doorway; the door indeed is the lodge's mouth.

On sunny days these strings were taken outside.   Several of the long poles, or drying rods, already described, were brought down from the top of the stage and lashed to the outside of the stage posts on either side. If the harvest was a good one, a row of these rods might extend the whole length of either side of the stage, and even around the ends.   On the railing thus made the squash strings were taken out and hung on a fair day; in the morning, on the east side; in the afternoon, on the west side of the stage.

On wet days, the squash strings were left inside the lodge; and if the rain was falling heavily, a tent skin, or scraped rawhides, dried and ready to tan, were thrown over them to protect from dampness. The air in the lodge was damp on a rainy day; and sometimes the roof leaked.

When the strings of squash were thought to be thoroughly dried, they were ready for storing. A portion was packed in parfleche bags, to be taken to the winter lodge, or to be used for food on journeys. The rest was stored away in a cache pit, covered with loose corn.

Several seasons, as I recollect, the women of my father's family were a month harvesting and drying their squashes.

Squash Blossoms

Besides our squashes, we also gathered squash blossoms, three to five basketfuls at a picking; and they were a recognized part of our squash harvest.

On every squash vine are blossoms of two kinds: one kind bears a squash, but the other never bears any fruit, for it grows, as we Indians say, at the wrong place among the leaves. We Indians knew this, and gathered only these barren blossoms; if we did not they dried up anyway and became a dead loss, so we always gathered them.

These blossoms we picked in early morning while they were fresh, but not if rain had fallen in the night, as the rain splashed dirt and sand into the blossoms, making them unfit for food.

The blossoms we took home in baskets. On the prairie there is a kind of grass which we Indians call "antelope hair." We chose a place where this grass grew thick and was two or three inches high, to dry the blossoms on. They were taken out of the basket one by one; the green calyx leaves were stripped off and the blossom was pinched flat, opened, and spread on the grass, with the inside of the blossom upward, thus exposing it to the sun and air. A second blossom was split on one side, opened, and laid upon the first, upon the petal end, so that the thicker, bulbous part of the first—the part indeed that had been pinched flat—remained exposed to dry. This was continued until quite a space on the grass was covered with the blossoms.

They remained all day drying. In the evening I would go out and gather them, pulling them up in whole sheets. Splitting them open and laying them down one upon another, caused them to adhere as they dried, so that they lay on the grass in a kind of thin matting. I always began pulling up the blossoms from one side of this matting, and as I say, they came away in whole sheets.

We put away the dried blossoms in bags, like those used for corn. These bags were made with round bottom and soft-skin mouth that tied easily. Bags were usually made of calf skin.

In my father's family we always put away one sack full of dried squash blossoms for winter.

Cooking and Uses of Squash

The First Squashes

The first squashes of the season that we plucked were about three inches in diameter; that is, they were gathered as soon as we thought they were fit for cooking; and that same day we picked blossoms also.

There might be three or four basketfuls of squashes at this first picking. These squashes we did not dry, but ate fresh; as they were the first vegetables of the season, we were eager to eat them. We cooked fresh squashes as follows:

Figure 22
Redrawn from sketch by Goodbird.

Boiling Fresh Squash in a Pot. I took a clay pot of our native manufacture, partly filled it with fresh squashes and added water. The smaller squashes I put in whole; larger ones I cut in two. I did not remove the seeds; left in the squash they made it taste sweeter.

I now took big leaves of the sunflower and thrust them, stem upward, between the squashes and the sides of the pot; the leaves then stood in a circle around the inside of the pot, with the upper surface of each leaf inward. I added more squashes until the pot was quite full, even heaping. The sunflower leaves I then bent inward, folding them naturally over the squashes. I now set the pot on the fire.

Under my direction Goodbird has made a sketch of a pot of fresh squashes (figure 22); the sunflower leaves are placed and ready to be folded down.

Squashes thus prepared were boiled a little longer than beef is boiled. The sunflower leaves were put over the pot merely as a lid or covering. It is hard to cook squashes without a cover, and this was our way of providing one. Blossoms were not added when squashes were thus prepared.

When the cooking was done, the green sunflower leaves, used as a cover, were removed with a stick, and thrown away.

I had a bowl of cold water near by. I dipped my hand into the water and lifted out the squash pieces one by one, and laid them on a bowl or dish. The cold water protected my hand; for the squashes were quite hot.

Most of the water in the pot had boiled out, only a little being left in the bottom of the pot. The pieces of squash immersed in this hot water I lifted out with a horn spoon. Not much water was ever put in the pot anyhow, for it was the steam mostly that cooked the squashes. The pot was quite heaped with squashes at the first, but the cooking reduced the bulk, making the heap go down.

The squash pieces in the bottom of the pot were apt to be a little burned or browned; and so were made sweeter, and were very good to eat.

This was the way we cooked fresh squashes in my father's family until I was eighteen years old; at that time we got an iron dinner pot, and began to boil our food in it instead of the old fashioned clay pot.

Fresh squashes, to be at their best, should be cooked on the day they are picked; left over to the next day they never taste so good.

Squashes Boiled with Blossoms. Fresh squashes were sometimes boiled with fresh blossoms and fats. Sunflower leaves were not then used as a covering. Squashes so cooked were usually small; and when done, they were lifted out of the pot with a horn spoon. Cooking this mess was really by boiling, not steaming, as in the mess above described.

Other Blossom Messes

When I wanted to cook fresh squash blossoms, I plucked them early in the morning, stripping them of the little points, or spicules shown as *a*, *a'*, and *a''* in figure 23. These spicules I stripped backward, or downward. I do not know why we did this; it was our custom. Then I broke the blossom off the stem at the place in the figure marked with a dotted line. The green bulbous part of the blossom I crushed or pinched between my thumb and finger, to make it soft and hasten cooking; for the yellow, blossom part soon cooked.

Figure 23

I will now give you recipes for some messes made with these fresh, crushed, spicule-stripped blossoms; however, dried blossoms were often used in these messes instead, and were just as good.

Boiled Blossoms. A little water was brought to boil in a clay pot. A handful of blossoms, either fresh or dried, was tossed into the pot and stirred with a stick. They shrunk up quite small, and another handful of blossoms was tossed in. This was continued until a small basketful of the blossoms had been stirred into the pot.

Into this a handful of fat was thrown, or a little bone grease was poured in; and the mess was let boil a little longer than meat is boiled, and a little less than fresh squash is boiled. The mess was then ready to eat.

Blossoms Boiled with Mądąpo′zi I′ti′a. Mądąpo′zi i′ti′a was made, the pot being put on the fire in the early afternoon and boiled for the rest of the day. In the night following the fire would go out and the mess would get cold.

In the morning the pot was set on the fire again, and if I was going to use fresh blossoms I went out to the field to gather them, expecting to return and find the pot heated and ready.   The newly gathered blossoms, crushed as described, I dropped in the rewarmed mess, and boiled for half an hour, when the pot was taken off, and the mess was served.

Sometimes this mess was further varied by adding beans.

Blossoms Boiled with Māpi' Nakapa'.   The blossoms were first boiled. Meal of pounded parched corn and fats were then added and the whole was boiled for half an hour.

Like the previous mess, this was sometimes varied by adding beans.

Seed Squashes

Selecting for Seed

Seed squashes were chosen at the first or second picking of the season. At these pickings, as we went from hill to hill plucking the four-days-old squashes, we observed what ones appeared the plumpest and finest; and these we left on the vine to be saved for seed.   We never chose more than one squash in a single hill; and to mark where it lay, and even more, to protect it from frost, we were careful to pull up a weed or two, or break off a few squash leaves and lay them over the squash; and thus protected, it was left on the vine.

There was a good deal of variety in our squashes.   Some were round, some rather elongated, some had a flattened end; some were dark, some nearly white, some spotted; some had a purple, or yellow top.   We did not recognize these as different strains, as we did the varieties of corn; and when I selected squashes for seed, I did not choose for color, but for size and general appearance.   Squashes of different colors grew in the same hill; and all varieties tasted exactly alike.

In later pickings, while we continued to gather the four-days-old squashes we did not disturb the seed squashes.   They were easily avoided, for if not plainly marked by the leaves I have said we laid over them, they could be recognized by their greater size, and their rough rind.   A four-days-old squash is smaller and has a smoother rind than a mature squash.

Gathering the Seed Squashes

The time for plucking the seed squashes was after we had gathered the first ripe corn, but had not yet gathered our seed corn.   It was our custom to pluck our corn until the first frost fell; then to gather our seed squashes; and afterwards our seed corn.   Some years the first frost fell very early, before we had plucked our first corn; in such seasons we gathered our seed squashes first, for we never let them lie in the field after the first frost had set in.

On this reservation the first frost falls at the end of the moon following this present moon.   We Indians call the present moon the wild cherry moon, because June berries ripen in the first half, and choke-cherries in the second half of the moon; and we reckon June berries as a kind of cherry. Our next moon we call the harvest moon; and in it wild plums ripen and the first frost falls.

The seed squashes when plucked, were all taken into the earth lodge and laid in a pile, on a bench. The bench was made of planks split from cottonwood trunks, laid lengthwise with the lodge wall. The squashes were piled in a heap on this bench; they were bigger than four-days-old squashes and their rinds were rougher and hard, like a shell.

Cooking the Ripe Squashes

When now we wanted to have squash for a meal, I went over to this heap of ripe seed squashes and brought a number over near the fire. There I broke them open, carefully saving the seeds. I would lay a squash on the floor of the lodge; with an elk horn scraper I would strike the squash smart blows on the side, splitting it open.

The broken half rinds I piled up one above another, concave side down, until ready to put them in the pot. Ripe squashes were less delicate than green four-days-old squashes, and did not spoil so quickly.

I was able to boil about ten ripe squashes in our family pot; but it took three such cookings of ten squashes each to make a mess for our family, which I have said was a large one. We boiled these ripe squashes like the four-days-old, in a very little water.

Saving the Seed

Always near the fireplace in our lodge there lay a piece of scraped hide about two feet square. It had many uses. When boiling meat we would lift the steaming meat from the pot and lay it on the hide before serving. We also used the hide for a drying cloth.

This piece of hide I drew near me when I was breaking ripe squashes; and as I removed the seeds I laid them in a pile on the hide. Squash seeds, freshly removed from the squash, are moist and mixed with more or less pulpy matter. To remove this pulp I took up a small handful of the fresh seeds, laid a dry corn cob in my palm and alternately squeezed and opened my hand over the mess. The porous surface of the cob absorbed the moisture and sucked up the pulpy matter, thus cleansing the seeds. As the cleansed seeds fell back upon the hide I took up another handful and repeated the process.

If there was a warm autumn sun, I often carried the hide with the cleansed seeds upon it, and laid it on the floor of the drying stage outside for the seeds to dry; but if the day was chill or winter had set in, I dried the seeds by the fire.

When quite dried, the seeds were put in a skin sack to be stored in a cache pit. The storing bag was often the whole skin of a buffalo calf, with only the neck left open for a mouth; or it might be made of a small fawn skin; or it might be made of a piece of old tent cover and shaped like a cylinder.

Eating the Seeds

Sometimes we boiled ripe squashes whole, seeds and all; and we then ate the seeds. They tasted something like peanuts.

These seeds of boiled squashes were eaten just as they came from the squash. I would take up two or three seeds in my mouth, crushing them with my teeth; and with my tongue I would separate the kernels from the shells which I spat out. I was rather fond of squash seeds.

I have also heard of families who prepared squash seeds by parching or roasting; but I never did this myself.

Roasting Ripe Squashes

I have heard that in old days my tribe used to roast fall-kept ripe squashes. They were buried in the ashes and roasted whole. I never did this myself, however.

There is a story that an old man who was blind, was handed a squash thus roasted. He found the squash to his liking, but did not know how it had been cooked.

"Girl," he cried, "let me have the broth this was boiled in!"

"The squash was roasted in the ashes; it has no broth," answered the girl who had handed it to him.

The blind man laughed. "I thought it was boiled in a pot," he said.

I judge from this story that several squashes had been roasted, and that the blind man got one as his share.

Storing the Unused Seed Squashes

It was our custom to remove to our winter village in the mida'-pạxi'di widi'c, or leaf-turn-yellow moon; it corresponds about to October. I remember the leaves used to be falling from the trees while we were working about our winter lodges, getting ready for cold weather.

When moving time came in the fall, any squashes left over in the lodge, uneaten, were stored in a cache pit until spring. But it was a difficult thing to store these squashes so that they would keep sound; and when spring came many of them would be found to have rotted. Some families were more careful in making ready and storing their cache pits than were others. Squashes kept best when stored in carefully prepared pits.

On the family's return the next spring the cache pit was opened; and the squashes that had kept sound could be used for cooking, and their seeds could be planted. The number thus stored over winter was not large.

The seeds of rotted squashes were just as good to plant as were the seeds of the sound squashes.

We carried no squash seeds with us to our winter village. For our spring planting we depended on the seed we had left stored in the cache in our summer lodge, in my father's family.

The seeds of a ripe squash are swelled and plump in the center; those of a four-days-old squash are flat. We could tell in this way if squash seeds were ripe.

Squashes, Present Seed

I grew our native squashes in my son Goodbird's garden until four years ago. I stopped cultivating them because my son's family did not seem to care to eat them. Last year a squash vine came up wild in my son's garden. The squashes that grew on it were of two colors. I saved some of the seed and planted them this year. It is from their yield that I have given you seed.

As I have said, squashes were of different colors and varied a good deal in shape; yet we recognized but one strain of seed. "We plant but one kind of seed," we said, "and all colors and shapes grow from it, dark, white, purple, round, elongated."

Squash Dolls

There is one other thing I will tell before we forsake the subject of squashes. Little girls of ten or eleven years of age used to make dolls of squashes.

When the squashes were brought in from the field, the little girls would go to the pile and pick out squashes that were proper for dolls. I have done so, myself. We used to pick out the long ones that were parti-colored; squashes whose tops were white or yellow and the bottoms of some other color. We put no decorations on these squashes that we had for dolls. Each little girl carried her squash about in her arms and sang for it as for a babe. Often she carried it on her back, in her calf skin robe.

CHAPTER VI

BEANS

Planting Beans

Bean planting followed immediately after squash planting.

Beans were planted in hills the size and shape of squash hills, or about seven by fourteen inches; but if made in open ground the hills were not placed so far apart in the row. Squash hills, like corn hills, stood about four feet apart in the row, measuring from center to center; but bean hills might be placed two feet or less in the row.

Beans, however, were very commonly planted not in open ground, but between our rows of corn; the hills were arranged as shown in diagram (figure 8, page 25).

Corn hills, I have said, stood four feet, or a little less in the row, and the rows were about four feet apart,[1] when corn was planted by itself. But if beans were to be planted between, the corn rows were placed a little farther apart, to make room for the bean hills.

Putting in the Seeds

To make a hill for beans, I broke up and loosened the soil with my hoe, scraping away the dry top soil; the hill I then made of the soft, slightly moist under-soil. The hill, as suggested by the measurements, was rather elongated.

I took beans, three in each hand, held in thumb and first two fingers, and buried them in a side of the hill, two inches deep, by a simultaneous thrust of each hand, as I stooped over; the two groups of seeds were six inches apart.

I have heard that some families planted four seeds in each group, instead of three; but I always put in three seeds and think that the better way. Figure 24 will explain the two ways of planting.

I am not sure that I know just why we planted beans always in the side of the hill; I have said we planted squash thus because the sprouted seeds were tender and the soil in the side of the hill did not bake hard after a rain. Also, we were careful not to make our bean hills too large, as the heavy rains turned the soft soil into mud which beat down over the vines, killing them.

[1] Measuring from center of corn hill to center of next corn hill.—G. L. W.

Hoeing and Cultivating

These subjects I have sufficiently described, I think, when I told you how we hoed and cultivated corn.

Threshing

Threshing was in the fall, after the beans had ripened and the pods were dead and dried. Sometimes, when the weather had been favorable, the bean vines were quite dry and could be threshed the same day they were gathered. But if the weather was a little damp, or if, as was usually the case, the vines were still a little green, they had to be dried a day or two before they could be threshed.

To prepare for this labor, I went out into the field and pulled up all the corn stalks in a space four or five yards in diameter; this was for a drying place.

I pulled up the vines of one bean hill and transferred them to my left hand, where I held them by the roots; I gathered another bunch of bean vines in my right hand, as many as I could conveniently carry; and I took these vines, borne in my two hands, to the drying place, and laid them on the ground, roots up, spreading them out a little. I thus worked until I had pulled up all the vines that grew near the drying place.

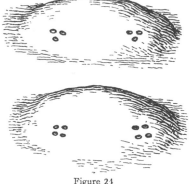

Figure 24
Redrawn from sketch by Goodbird.

I made several such drying places, as the need required; and on them I put all the bean vines to dry.

At the end of about three days, when the vines were dry I took out into the field half of an old tent cover and laid it on the ground in an open space made by clearing away the corn stalks. This tent cover, so laid, was to be my threshing floor.

We never laid this tent cover at the edge of the field on the grass, because in threshing the vines, some of the beans would fly up and fall outside the tent cover, on the ground. We always picked these stray beans up carefully, after threshing. This could not be done if we threshed on the grass.

My threshing floor ready, I took up some of the dry vines and laid them on the tent cover in a heap, about three feet high. I got upon this heap with my moccasined feet and smartly trampled it, now and then standing on one foot, while I shuffled and scraped the other over the dry vines; this was done to shake the beans loose from their pods.

When the vines were pretty well trampled I pushed them over two or three feet to one side of the tent cover; and having fetched fresh vines, I made another heap about three feet high, which also I trampled and pushed aside.   When I had trampled three or four heaps in this manner I was ready to beat them.

We preferred to tread out our beans thus, because beating them with a stick made the seeds fly out in all directions upon the ground; when the vines were trampled, this would not happen.   However, after the treading was over, there were always a few unopened pods still clinging to the vines; and to free the beans from these pods, we beat the vines at the end of every three or four treadings.

This beating I did with a stick, about the size of the stick used as a flail in threshing corn.

I always threshed my beans on a windy day if possible, so that I might winnow them immediately after the threshing.   If the wind died down, I covered over the threshed beans and waited until the wind came up again. A small carrying basket or a wooden bowl, was used to winnow with.

After the beans were winnowed, they were dried one more day, either on a tent cover in the garden, or at home on a skin placed on the ground near the drying stage.   At the end of this day's drying, they were ready to be packed in sacks.

Our bean harvests varied a good deal from year to year; in my father's family, from as little as half a sack, to as much as three barrels.   The biggest harvest our family ever put up, that I remember, was equivalent to about three barrelfuls.   Of course we did not use barrels in those days.

Bean threshing never lasted long; it was work that could be done rapidly.

Gathering up the vines, threshing, and winnowing took about a day and a half; the actual threshing lasted only about half a day.   But this does not take into account the time the vines and the threshed beans lay drying.

I remember that one year, when our crop was of good size, for the whole work of threshing and labor of getting our bean crop in, I spent but three days.   In this time I had gathered up the vines, threshed them, and winnowed the threshed beans.

However, the time necessary for these labors varied much with the crop, the weather, and the greenness of the vines.

Varieties

There were five varieties of beans in common use in my tribe, as follows:

Ama′ca ci′pica . . .	Black bean
Ama′ca hi′ci	Red bean
Ama′ca pu′xi . . .	Spotted bean
Ama′ca ita′ wina′ki matu′hica	Shield-figured bean
Ama′ca ata̜′ki . . .	White bean

These varieties we planted, each by itself; and each kind, again, was kept separate in threshing; also, only beans of the same variety were put in one bag for storing. Black, red, white, shield-figured, spotted, each had a separate bag.

Besides the foregoing varieties, there were some families who raised a variety of yellow beans. I once planted some seed of this variety, but did not find that they bred very true to color; I do not know if this was because I did not get very good seed.

I do not think these yellow beans were in use in my tribe in very old times. Whether they were imported to us by white men, or, as seems likely, were brought from other tribes, I do not know.

The white beans now raised in this part of the reservation, seed of which you have purchased, is from white man's stock. The seed was brought to us, I think, when I was a little girl, or about sixty years ago. But we Hidatsas and Mandans had white beans before this. The two strains are easily distinguished. In the white man's variety, the eye is a little sunken in the seed. In the native white beans, the eye is on a level with the body of the bean.

Selecting Seed Beans

In the spring, when I came to plant beans, I was very careful to select seed for the following points: seed should be fully ripe; seed should be of full color; seed should be plump, and of good size.

If the red was not a deep red, or the black a deep black, I knew the seed was not fully ripe, and I would reject it. So also of the white, the spotted, and the shield-figured.

Did I learn from white men thus to select seed? (Laughing heartily.) No, this custom comes down to us from very old times. We were always taught to select seed thus, in my tribe.

White men do not seem to know very much about raising beans. Our school teacher last year raised beans in a field near the school-house; and when harvest time came, he tried to pluck the pods directly into a basket, without treading or threshing the vines. I think it would take him a very long time to harvest his beans in that manner.

Cooking and Uses

Of the several varieties, I like to eat black beans best. Especially I like to use black beans in making mä'dakapa. However, all the other kinds were good.[2]

[2] "I have raised white beans mostly of late years because it is easier to sell them to white men. This summer, however (1913), I planted several acres also to other kinds of our Hidatsa beans, red, black, spotted.

"I find that the black beans have yielded best, next the red, then the spotted, last of all the white. I have observed before that this is true; that black beans yield the most."—WOLF CHIEF

I have already described to you some of the dishes we made, and still make, with beans.   Following are some messes I have not described:

Ama'ca Di'hĕ, or *Beans-Boiled*.   The beans were boiled in a clay pot, with a piece of buffalo fat, or some bone grease.   If the beans were dried beans, they were boiled a little longer than squash is boiled—a half hour or more.   Spring salt, or other seasoning, was not used.

Green beans, shelled from the pod, were sometimes prepared thus, boiled with buffalo fat or bone grease; but green beans did not have to be boiled quite as long as dried beans.

Green Beans Boiled in the Pod.   Green beans in the pod we boiled and ate as a vegetable from the time they came in until fall; but we did not plant beans, as we did corn, to make them come in late in the season, that we might then eat them green.

Green beans in the pod were boiled in a clay pot, with a little fat thrown in.   Pods and seeds were eaten together.

But a green bean pod has in it two little strings that are not very good to eat.   At meal time the boiled pod was taken up in the fingers and carried to the eater's mouth.   At one end of the pod is always a kind of little hook; the unbroken pod was taken into the mouth with this little hook forward, between the teeth; and the eater, seizing the little hook between thumb and finger, drew it out of his mouth with the two little strings that were always attached to the hook.

Green Corn and Beans.   Pounded green shelled corn was often boiled with green beans, shelled from the pod.

CHAPTER VII

STORING FOR WINTER

The Cache Pit

We stored our corn, beans, sunflower seed and dried squash in cache pits for the winter, much as white people keep vegetables in their cellars.

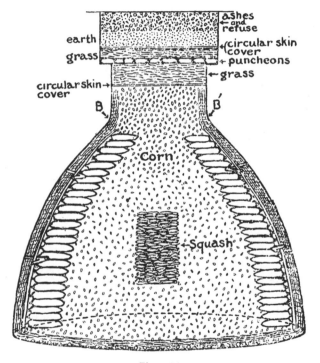

Figure 25
Redrawn from sketch by Goodbird.

A cache pit was shaped somewhat like a jug, with a narrow neck at the top. The width of the mouth, or entrance, was commonly about two feet; on the very largest cache pits the mouth was never, I think, more than two feet eight, or two feet nine inches. In diagram (figure 25), the width of pit's mouth at *BB'* should be a little more than two feet, narrowing to two feet a little higher up.

In my father's family, we built our cache pits so that they were each of the size of a bull boat at the bottom. Other measurements were, as

I here show with my hands, one foot eight inches from the top of the mouth, where it is level with the ground, down to the puncheon cover that lay in the trench dug for the purpose; and two feet and a half from this plank cover to the lower part of the neck, marked *BB'* in the diagram.

Descent into one of these big cache pits was made with a ladder; but in a small one, such as I have made you in vertical-section model, in a bank by the Missouri, and which you have photographed, the depth was not so great. In one of these smaller pits, when standing on the floor within, my eyes just cleared the level of the ground above, so that I could look around. When such a pit was half full of corn, I could descend and come out again, without the help of a ladder. At other times I had to be helped out; I would hold up my hands, and my mother, or some one else, would come and give me a lift.

Usually, two women worked together thus in a cache pit, one helping the other out, or taking things from her hands. One of my mothers was usually my helper.

The digging and storing of a cache pit was women's work. For digging the pit, a short handled hoe was used; of iron, in my day; of bone, I have heard, in olden times.

I have dug more than one cache pit myself. I began by digging the round mouth, dragging the loosened earth away with my hoe. As the pit grew in depth, the excavated earth was carried off in a wooden bowl. I stood in the pit with the bowl at my feet and labored with my hoe, raking the earth into the bowl. When it was full, I handed the bowl to my mother, who bore it away and emptied it.

It took me two days and a good part of a third to dig a cache pit, my mother helping me to carry off the dirt; such a cache pit, I mean, as we used in my father's family, and which, as I have said, was large enough for a bull boat cover to be fitted into the bottom.

A trench for the puncheon cover of the mouth was the very last part of the cache pit to be dug; but I will describe the use of this trench a little farther on.

Grass for Lining

When the cache pit was all dug, it had next to be lined with grass The grass used for this purpose, and for closing the mouth of the cache pit, was the long bluish kind that grows near springs and water courses on this reservation; it grows about three feet high. In the fall, this kind of grass becomes dry at the top, but is still green down near the roots; and we then cut it with hoes and packed it in bundles, to the village.

This bluish grass was the only kind used for lining a cache pit. We knew by repeated trials that other kinds of grass would mold, and did not keep well.

Grass Bundles

I remember, one time, I went out with my mother to cut grass. I took a pony along to pack our loads home. I loaded the pony with four bundles of grass, two on each side, bound to the saddle. A bundle was about four feet long, and from two and a half to three feet thick, pressed tight together. One bundle made a load for a woman.

Besides the four bundles loaded on my pony, my mother packed one bundle back to the village, and three or four dogs dragged each a bundle on a travois.

We reckoned that three of these bundles would be needed to line and close a large cache pit; and two and a half bundles, for a smaller pit. A hundred such bundles were needed to cover the roof of an earth lodge. Long established use made us able to make the bundles about alike in weight, though of course we had no scales to weigh them in those days.

The Grass Binding Rope

Each bundle was bound with a rope of grass. In a bed of this grass as it stands by the spring or stream, there is often found dead grass from the year before, or even from two years previous, standing among the other grass stems that are still somewhat green at the roots. To make a binding rope I must use only dead grass. I did so in this manner:

I stooped, took a wisp of grass in my hands, twisting it to the left and at the same gently lifting it, when all the dry stems would break off at the roots. I took a half step forward, laid the twisted end of the strand on the ground, and grasped another wisp of grass, which I twisted to the left and broke off as before; but I twisted the new wisp in such manner that it made part of the continued twisted strand. I continued thus until I had a strand long enough to tie my bundle. Figure 26 is a sketch made after my description of a grass bundle, showing the grass rope and the tie.

Drying the Grass Bundles

These grass bundles we fetched home and laid on the drying stage until we were ready to use them. Just before using, we took the bundles up on the roof of the earth lodge, broke the binding ropes and spread the grass out to dry, for one day.

The Willow Floor

The walls of the cache pit were left bare for the grass lining; but a floor was laid on the bottom. This was rather simply made by gathering dead and dry willow sticks, and laying them evenly and snugly over the bottom of the pit.

The Grass Lining

Over this willow floor, the grass, now thoroughly dried, was spread evenly, to a depth of about four inches. Grass was then spread over

the walls to a depth of three or four inches, and stayed in place with about eight willow sticks. These were placed vertically against the walls and nailed in place with wooden pins made each from the fork of a dead willow, as shown in figure 27. The ends of the sticks should reach to the neck of the cache pit, at the place marked *B*, in diagram (figure 25, page 87).

Figure 26

Exact reproduction of sketch by Goodbird. The tie is pronounced accurate by Buffalobird-woman.

We were careful to spread the grass lining evenly over the walls; and we were especially careful not to let the root ends get matted together, as they were very apt to do.

It will be noticed that the willow flooring of the pit, the willow staying rods, and the wooden pins that held them in place, were all made of dead and dry willows; this was done that everything within the pit might be perfectly dry.

It did not take long to place the grass lining of the cache pit.

Skin Bottom Covering

If the cache pit was a small one, we covered the bottom with a circular piece of skin, cut to fit the pit bottom, and laid it directly on the grass matting that covered the willow floor; but if the cache pit was a large one, we fitted into the bottom the skin cover of a bull boat, with the willow frame removed.

Storing the Cache Pit

The cache pit was now ready to be stored.

My mother and I—and by "my mother" I mean always one of my two mothers, for my mother that bore me was dead—fetched an old tent cover from the earth lodge, and laid it by the cache pit so that one end of the cover hung down the pit's mouth.

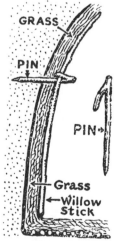

Figure 27

Upon this tent cover we emptied a big pile of shelled ripe corn, fetched in baskets from the bull boats in which it had been temporarily stored inside the lodge. We also fetched many strings of braided corn, and laid

them on one side of the tent cover.   Lastly, we fetched some strings of
dried squash and laid them on the tent cover.

Of dried squash, I fetched but one string at a time, doubled and folded
over my left arm.   A string of dried squash, as I have said, was always
seven Indian fathoms long; and I have described an Indian fathom as the
distance from the tips of the fingers of one hand to the tips of the fingers
of the other, with both hands outstretched at either side.   As these measurements were made by the women workers, an Indian fathom averaged
about five and a half feet in length.   A string of dried squash, seven Indian

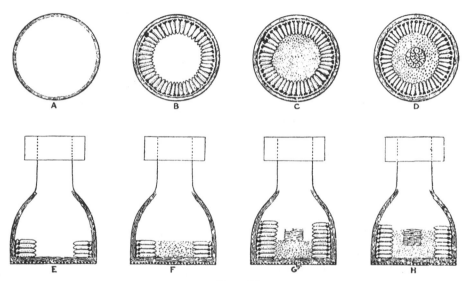

Figure 28
Plan of cache in horizontal section: A, floor ready for storing; B, the first series of braided strings;
C, loose corn; D, first squash string.
In vertical section: E, the first series of braided strings of corn; F, adding loose corn; G, the first
squash string; H, loose corn filled in around squash.

fathoms in length, we knew by experience to be just about the weight that
a woman could conveniently carry.   A string eight fathoms long would
be too heavy; and one six fathoms long would be rather short.

All being now ready, my mother descended into the cache pit.   Leaning over the mouth, I handed her a string of braided corn.   In my father's
family, we usually braided fifty-four, or fifty-five ears, to a string; and a
woman could carry about three strings on her left shoulder.   These braided
strings, as I have said, my mother and I fetched from the drying stage;
she stood on the stage floor and handed me the braided strings, and I bore
them off to the cache pit.

Leaning over the pit then, as I have said, I handed my mother one of
the braided strings that now lay in a heap on the tent cover.   My mother

took the string of corn, folded it once over, and laid it snugly against the wall of the cache pit, on the skin bottom covering, with the tips of the ears all pointed inward. Folding a string thus kept the ears from slipping, and stayed them more firmly in place; and the ears, laid husk end to the wall, were better preserved from danger of moisture.

My mother continued thus all around the bottom of the pit, until she had surrounded it with a row of braided corn laid against the wall, two ears deep; for the strings, being doubled, lay therefore two ears deep.

My mother now started a second row, or series, of strings of braided corn doubled over, laying them upon the first series; and like these, with the ears all pointed inward. When this series was completed, the bottom of the cache pit was surrounded by strings of braided corn, which, because doubled, now lay four ears deep.

My mother now called to me that she was ready for the shelled, or loose, corn. Obeying her, I pushed the shelled corn that lay on the tent cover, down the overhanging end of the skin into the cache pit, until the floor of the pit was filled up level with the top of the four-tiered series of strings of braided corn. It will be seen now how necessary it was that a hide or bull boat cover be put in the bottom of the cache pit, to receive this shelled grain.

I next passed down a string of dried squash, seven fathoms long; and this my mother coiled and piled up in the center of the cache pit upon the shelled corn. This loose corn, I have already said, lay level with the top-most row of ears laid against the pit's wall, but did not quite cover the ears. I remember, as I looked down into the pit, I could see these corn ears lying in a circle about the loose corn within. Figure 28, drawn under my direction, shows in a series of rough sketches how the cache pit was filled.

Again I passed down strings of braided corn to my mother. These she doubled, as before, and laid them around the wall of the cache pit, until they came up level with the top of the squash heap coiled in the center. We did not have any fixed number of rows of corn to place now; my mother just piled the doubled braids around the wall until they came even with the top of the coiled squash string.

My mother then called to me, and again I shoved loose corn into the cache pit, until it just barely covered the coiled squash pile and the top-most row of braided ears.

The object of our putting the squash in the center of the shelled corn was to protect it from dampness. The shelled ripe corn did not spoil very easily, but dried squash did. We were careful, therefore, to store the strings of squash in the very center of the cache pit and surround them on every side with the loose corn; this protected the squash and kept it dry.

We continued working, my mother and I, until the cache pit was filled. In an average sized cache pit we would usually store four seven-fathom strings of dried squash, coiled each in a heap in the center of the cache and hidden as described, in the loose corn; and as I recollect it, I think it took about thirty or more strings of braided corn to lie around the wall of an average sized pit; but my memory here is a little uncertain, and this estimate may not be quite accurate.

We filled the pit about up to the point marked *B* in the diagram (figure 25), the last two feet being filled with shelled corn only; thus the last string of squash put in the cache pit should be covered with at least two feet of loose corn.

Over this shelled corn, at *B* in the diagram, we snugly fitted a circular cover, cut from the thick skin of the flank of a buffalo bull. A bull's hide is thicker than a buffalo cow's, and for this reason was seldom made into a robe; but there were purposes for which a bull's hide was preferred. Thus the heavy thick-haired parts of a bull's hide were much used for making saddle skins, because the heavy wool protected the horse's back; and the short haired parts were much used for making cache pit covers. Using these parts of the hide for covers, we did not have to bother to scrape off the hair, which in summer is very short on a buffalo's flanks. The skin cover was laid hair side up, so that the flesh side would come next to the loose corn.

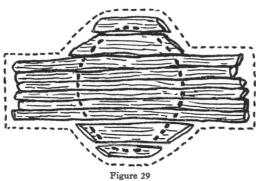

Figure 29
Redrawn from sketch by Goodbird.

On this hide cover my mother and I laid grass,[1] of the same kind as used for lining the cache pit wall.

The Puncheon Cover

Upon this grass, if the pit was one of the smaller ones, we laid puncheons; and these puncheons, as I have said, rested in a trench.

The puncheons, split from small logs, were laid in the trench flat side down, so that they would not rock. There were about five main planks, or puncheons, the middle one being the heaviest, the better to sustain the weight of any horse that might happen to walk over the cache pit's mouth. On either side of these main puncheons were two shorter ones, laid to cover the small area of the pit's mouth not covered by the main puncheons.

Figure 29 by Goodbird, drawn from the small model I made for you in Wolf Chief's yard, will explain this. The puncheons shown in the figure

[1] Slough grass, a species of Spartina.

exactly fit the trench; and their circumscribed outline represents also the
shape of the trench.   The dotted circle represents the pit's mouth, now
hidden by the over-lying puncheons.

Upon the puncheons we now laid grass, quite filling the pit's mouth,
and even heaped, it might be, a foot high above the level of the ground;
this we trampled down hard, well into the mouth of the pit.

Over this grass we fitted a second cover, cut as was the first from a
buffalo bull's hide; and upon this we heaped earth until the pit was filled
level with the ground.

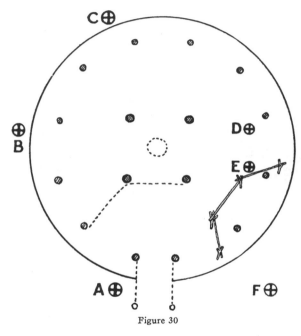

Figure 30

Lastly, we raked ashes and refuse dirt over the spot, to hide it from any
enemy that might come prowling around in the winter, when the village
was deserted.

I have said that puncheons, resting in a trench, were used to cover the
mouth of a cache pit of smaller size. If the pit was of the larger size, I dug
about two feet down in the neck or opening, a rectangular place on either
side, with my knife.   Puncheons were thrust down into one of these rectangular openings and drawn through into the other, covering the mouth
of the pit; and as in the smaller pit, there were several main puncheons,
with one or two smaller and shorter ones at either side.   Grass was stuffed
into the two openings, above the ends of the puncheons, to firm the latter.
Above the puncheons, the mouth of the pit was filled in, as was that of the
smaller pit, with grass, a circular skin cover, and earth.

The two rectangular openings which I dug with my knife in the neck of the larger pit, were, as will be noted, a little farther down than was the floor of the trench of the smaller pit. This was because the neck was longer in a pit of the larger size.

Cache Pits in Small Ankle's Lodge

First Account

In diagram (figure 30), I have marked the positions of the cache pits we had in use in my father's family, when I was a girl. Cache A was used for hard yellow shelled corn; but the braids piled against the wall of the pit were of white corn; so also of B and C. In cache D were stored dried boiled corn and strings of dried squash.

Sometimes in one of the cache pits outside of the lodge we put a bag of beans, or sometimes two bags. Each bag was of skin and was about as long as one's arm; its shape was long and round.

In the fall, when we went to our winter lodges, corn, squash, beans, and whatever else was needed, we loaded on our horses and took with us. As soon as we came to our winter lodge we made ready a cache pit at once and stored these things away.

We opened a cache pit whenever we got out of provisions. When should this be, you ask? When we got out of provisions. This might happen at any time. One winter, I remember, we got out of provisions and a number of our people left the winter village and went to the lodges at Like-a-fishhook village, to open a cache. The Sioux surrounded them there. Our people took refuge in a kind of fort that belonged to the traders and fired down from an upper room; they killed two of the Sioux.

Cache pit F in the diagram, we made afterwards. Pit E was also of later make; we dug it after we got potatoes; it was inside the lodge and near the corral for horses.

Cache pit C we had to abandon because mice got into it and we could not get rid of them. So we filled it up with earth and dug pit D. We stored gummy corn in cache pit D and used it for two years. The third year the Sioux came against our village in the winter time and stole our corn and burned down my father's lodge.

I have been telling you how the cache pit was used for storing things for winter; but I do not mean that it was of no use in summer time. In early spring we put into a cache pit two big packages of dried meat and a bladder full of bone grease. We did not take them out until about August or a little earlier. The meat would still be good, and the bone grease would be hard and sweet, just as if it were frozen.

A cache pit lasted for a long time, used year after year.

A Second Account on Another Day

We had four cache pits to store grain for my father's family; one held squash, vegetables, corn, etc.

A second held shelled yellow corn. In this cache the usual strings of corn laid around to protect the shelled grain from the wall, were of white corn. We did not braid hard yellow corn. It was corn that we did not often use for parching.

A third cache held white shelled corn, protected by the usual braided strings of white corn.

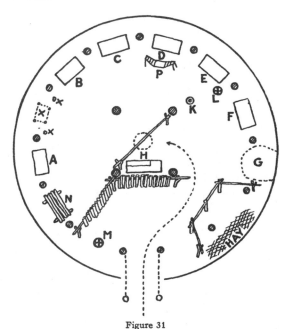

Figure 31

Redrawn from sketch by Goodbird.

A. Bed of Small Ankle and Strikes-many-women.

B. Bed of Wolf Chief and wife.

C. Bed of Bear's Tail and wife.

D. Bed of Son-of-a-Star and his wife Buffalo-bird-woman.

E. Bed of Flies-low, Yellow Front Hair and Fell-upon-his-house, three boys.

F. Bed of Turtle.

G. Place for storing ax, hay, wood, or any thing that could be piled or laid away.

H. Bed of Small Eyes, elder sister of Strikes-many-women; the bed here by the fire-place being the warmest was commonly reserved for an elderly person. (Small Eyes is probably the same as Red Blossom).

K. Corn mortar and pestle.

L. and M. Cache pits.

N. Platform of slabs on which were stored food, utensils, etc.

P. Lazy-back or native chair.

XXX. Small Ankle's medicines, or sacred objects.

A fourth cache pit was a small one inside the lodge; here we stored dried wild turnips, dried choke-cherries, and dried June berries; and any valuables that we could not take with us to our winter village.

Our cache pits were for the most part located outside the lodge, because mice were found inside the lodge, and they were apt to be troublesome.

In the cache pit where we stored our yellow corn, we stored the grain loose, not in sacks.

I knew of course where each cache pit was located.

The Sioux sometimes came up against us in winter and raided our cached corn.   One winter (about 1877) they came up and burned our lodges and stole all that was in our cache pits.

We returned from our winter quarters to our permanent village a little before ice breaks on the Missouri, or in the latter part of March.

Diagram of Small Ankle's Lodge

Figure 31 is a diagram of Small Ankle's lodge, as I remember it.   My three brothers slept in bed *E*, but often Wolf Chief or Bear's Tail and their wives would be away, staying at some other lodge, perhaps at the wife's mother's; sometimes they visited thus for a long time.   The boys might then make use of the vacant bed of the visiting couple.

All beds were covered with skins, as I have before described to you.

Small children slept with their parents.

I do not know why my father put his medicine shrines in the rear of the lodge.   Ours was a big family and there was not room enough for all the beds on one side.   Probably Small Ankle wanted the medicine objects near his bed and not where the children were.

CHAPTER VIII

THE MAKING OF A DRYING STAGE

Stages in Like-a-fishhook Village

There were about seventy lodges in Like-a-fishhook village, when I was a girl. A corn drying stage stood before every lodge.

That before Small Ankle's lodge was a three-section stage, of eight posts. White Feather, or his wives, owned two of these big eight-post stages, one before each of their two lodges; for White Feather had four wives. Many Growths—a woman—had a big eight-post stage. There were a few other eight-post stages in the village, but they were small, with narrow sections and posts placed relatively rather close to one another.

The rest of the stages in the village, as I recollect, were all six-post, or two-section, stages.

In all cases, whether of a six-post or eight-post stage, the floor was upheld by two long, but narrow beams, that ran the whole length of the stage.

The description I shall now give of the making of a drying stage, is of an eight-post stage, such as always stood before my father's lodge.

Cutting the Timbers

The timbers we used for building a drying stage were all of cottonwood. Being thus of a soft wood, the timbers did not last so very long when exposed to the weather; and a stage built of cottonwood timbers lasted only about three years; the fourth year, unless the stage was rebuilt, the posts rotted and the stage would fall down. Unlike the posts of a watchers' stage, those of a drying stage were always carefully peeled of bark, as they rotted more quickly if the bark was left on.

My mother's drying stage, as I have said, had eight posts; and these posts we cut with forks at the top. If we could find them, or if we had time to hunt for them in the woods, we cut double-forked posts, like that of figure 32. But it was much easier to get the smaller posts, of the height of the stage floor. Such a post had but one fork at the top, in which lay one of the beams that supported the floor; and a companion post, longer and not so heavy, stood by it to support the railing at the top of the stage. However, in reckoning the number of posts of a stage, I count a single-forked post and its companion as but one post.

For the two long beams on which the floor of the stage was to be laid, we cut two rather slender logs, the longest we could find in the woods.

All these timbers we cut in the summer time, peeling off the bark and letting them lie until winter, to dry. Then when there was snow on the ground, we hitched ropes to the seasoned timbers and dragged them into the village.

The stage was built the following spring or summer, to be ready for the fall harvest; so that we commonly cut the timbers for a stage nine months or a year before they were to be used in building it.

Digging the Post Holes

When we were ready to begin building, the first thing we had to do was to mark the post holes. We laid the two long floor beams parallel on the ground, at such a distance apart as to enclose the space necessary for the stage. We then marked the places for the post holes, at proper distances along the inside of the two beams; there were eight of these post holes, four on a side.

These post holes were dug with a long digging stick, and the dirt removed, to the depth of a woman's arm from the shoulder to the hand; that was as far as one could reach down to lift out the dirt. To get the post holes all of a depth, I took a stick and measured on it the length of my arm from shoulder to fingers; this stick I used to probe the holes to see that they were of a proper depth.

We now laid down all the posts in a row, and so adjusted them that the forks that were to receive the floor beams lay all in a straight line; that is, if the posts were two-forked posts, all the forks *C* (figure 32) would lie in a straight line; and if the posts, or some of them, were single-forked posts, their tops would lie in a line with fork *C* of the double-forked posts.

Figure 32

On all the posts a charcoal line was now drawn at *A* (figure 32). The distance from *A* to *B* (figure 32) should be the length of a woman's arm, which also was the depth of the post hole. But in cutting the posts, no matter how careful we were, there was always some irregularity in lengths so that the part from *A* to *B* upon the various posts might slightly vary.

All having now been marked with the charcoal line, the posts were rolled each to its proper post hole and the part *AB* on the post was carefully measured and compared with the hole's depth. For this purpose the stick used to probe the post holes came again into use. If the length of the part *AB* on any post happened to be an inch or two longer than my arm its post hole was deepened to the same extent. All this was necessary in order that when the posts were dropped into their holes. the forks that were to receive the floor beams would lie all at the same height.

I have said that a charcoal line was drawn around each post at *A* (figure 32). The position of this line, after the first one was drawn, was obtained by measuring from the fork *C*; and care was taken that the measurements on all the posts should be exactly alike. The charcoal line quite encircled the post.

Raising the Frame

The posts were now raised and dropped into the post holes; raising was by hand. The posts were turned so that the forks lay in proper position to receive the floor beams and upper rails; a two-forked post was placed with the prong *C* (figure 32) turned inward.

A single-forked post had to have a companion post beside it, also forked, to support the railing at the top of the stage. This companion post was not so heavy, but of course was longer. It stood just beside the main post and was carefully adjusted to receive the upper rail properly. It was lashed to the main post by a green-hide thong.

This thong might pass around the shorter post just below its fork; or it might bind the companion post to one of the prongs of the fork itself.

If I had several two-forked posts and several one-forked posts with companion posts beside them, it required some little bit of fitting to adjust them all so that the floor beams and rails would lie properly. To better permit this to be done, it was not my custom to firm the earth about the post, until the frame had been set up and adjusted; for little irregularities in the fitting could be cured by slightly moving the posts as they stood unfirmed, in their holes. When the frame was properly adjusted, I took my digging stick—it was always a long one that was used for digging holes—and rammed the earth around the foot of each post, firming it.

It was the custom of my tribe when digging the post holes, to dig each one just the diameter of its post, or as nearly to it as we could; then the posts when raised fitted snugly into the holes.

The two long floor beams having been raised into position, the two poles that were to make the top railing were also raised. These rails were of the same length, but were not so heavy, as the floor beams. We were now ready to lay the floor.

The Floor

The floor of the stage was of cottonwood planks. Cottonwood logs, nine to twelve inches in diameter, had been cut of proper length. Out of the center of each was split a plank, or board, with ax and wedge. These planks were laid to make the floor, the ends of the planks resting on the two floor beams that lay on the forks of the posts. We took care to make the floor as snug as possible. The planks were carefully fitted together, and if there was any little crooked place in a plank that left a crack in the floor, we stuffed a dry cornstalk into the crack so that no ear of corn could fall through.

The planks that made the floor were not bound to the floor beams, nor weighted down in any way; their own weight stayed them in place.

I have said that the drying stage had to be rebuilt about every three years because the posts rotted down in that time. This was not true of the floor planks; they lasted much longer and were used year after year.

Staying Thongs

The eight posts of the stage stood in pairs, a post on either side of the floor; and between the tops of each pair of posts a green-hide thong was bound, and left to dry. These thongs stayed the stage and made it stronger and firmer; often they were also made to bind down the upper rails to the forks of the posts.

Ladder

The stage stood always in front of the earth lodge with its longer side to the door. A ladder stood at the right hand nigher corner post—as one comes out of the lodge—with the foot of the ladder resting a little way from the stage. The top of the ladder leaned against the end of the floor beam on the side next the lodge.

Of course if the ladder were left here with nothing to stay it, it would fall against the loose planks of the stage floor and force them out of position. To prevent this a pole was bound firmly to the two posts *A* and *B* (figure 12) and resting on the two floor beams just outside the posts. The ladder rested against this pole. To receive the pole, the floor beams were made to project a little bit forward at the ladder end of the stage.

Ladder with details of the ends

Figure 33

The ladder was made of a cottonwood trunk, about ten inches in diameter, with notches cut in it for steps. At its lower end it was brought to an edge that it might more firmly rest on the ground and not turn when someone stepped on it. At the upper end a notch was cut in the back to receive the end of the floor beam against which the ladder rested. (See figure 33.)

The ladder had always one fixed place; or, if for any reason it had to be moved during labors, we took pains to warn our friends. A woman in our village once moved her ladder to another place on her stage and forgot about it. When she started to come down she stepped in the old place and fell and broke both her arms.   We did not like to have a ladder removed from its accustomed place for fear of just such accidents.

When the owner descended from her drying stage, she took down her ladder and laid it on the ground beside the stage.   It was not proper for strangers to go up on the drying stage, nor were children allowed to go up there.

Neighbors sometimes came in and borrowed the ladder; but when not in use, its proper place was on the ground by the stage.

You ask me how we Indian women ascended and descended a ladder. I never thought of our having any particular custom in this; but now that you call my attention to it, I remember that a woman ascended and descended a ladder with her face toward the stage, giving her the appearance of going up sidewise, and coming down in the same manner.

In going up a ladder I usually placed my left foot on the lowest step; brought my right foot around in front and over my left to the second step; then my left foot past and behind my right foot, with my face toward the drying stage.   My left hand might or might not touch the ladder, as I was used to ascending it and felt no fear.

In descending a ladder I placed my right foot on the highest step, and overlapped with my left; and so until the bottom was reached.

I do not know if other women had exactly this custom, for I never observed or thought anything about it; but I do know that always, ascending or descending, an Indian woman went sidewise, with her face toward the stage.

Enlarging the Stage

Some years, if our family's corn crop was very large, we extended our drying stage, making it five posts long instead of four posts long, on a side.   Other families did likewise, as they had need; one family might have corn enough to require a stage five posts long, while another family needed one only four posts long, on a side   Stages, indeed, varied in length with the needs of the family, but they were all of about the same width.

Present Stages

The stage that I have been describing is of the kind that was in use in my tribe when I was a young girl of twelve or thirteen years of age.   At present we no longer use this, our old form, but the Arikara form instead.

The Arikara stage differs in having a floor of willows, and is easier to make.   It took two days to erect a stage of the old fashioned kind, such as I have been describing.

Building, Women's Work

Building the drying stage was women's work, although the men helped raise the heavy posts and floor beams.   In my father's family, my two mothers and I built the stage; but my father also helped us, especially if there was any heavy lifting to do.

Measurements of Stage

I will now give you the measurements of such a stage as we used in my father's family.

Pacing it off here, on the ground, the length of the stage was, I think, about so long—thirty feet.[1] Its width was about thus—twelve feet. From the ground to the top of the stage floor was a little higher than a woman can reach with her hand, or about six feet, six inches; there were horses in the village, and the stage floor must be high enough so that the horses could not reach the corn. From the floor of the stage to the upper railing was about so high (holding up a stick), or five feet and nine inches.

I will now give you the measurements of the posts and beams; and for this, we will use the little model which I have made for you. In this model

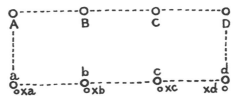

Figure 34

I have used double-forked posts on one side, and single-forked posts, with companion posts, on the other side.

In the diagram (figure 34), *A*, *B*, *C*, *D*, are double-forked posts; *a*, *b* *c*, *d*, are single-forked posts; and *xa*, *xb*, *xc*, *xd*, are companion posts.

The double-forked posts, *A*, *B*, *C*, and *D*, should be about ten inches in diameter between the lower fork and the ground, but tapering slightly toward the upper fork. This upper fork, if it was not in the post naturally, might be cut to receive the upper rail. The posts *a*, *b*, *c*, and *d*, should be ten inches in diameter; and the companion posts, *xa*, *xb*, *xc*, and *xd*, should be, perhaps, four inches in diameter. All of these posts are set in the ground with the smaller, or branch end upward.

The floor beams should each be about nine and one-half inches in diameter at one end, tapering to four or five inches in diameter at the other end. This tapering was the natural growth of the trunk; it was not, I mean, cut tapering with an ax. The beams were so laid that the heavy ends were always at the front of the stage as we called it; that is, at the end where the ladder stood.

[1] Buffalobird-woman here means a three-section stage. A stage of four sections would be forty feet or more in length.—G. L. W.

The upper rails were about three and a half inches in diameter. They were chosen for strength, if possible of trunks that were branchless, or nearly so. These upper rails were also laid with the heavy ends toward the front, or ladder end, of the stage.

I have said that if the long posts, *A*, *B*, *C*, *D*, had no natural fork at the top, one was cut; but all other forks, and those also on the tops of the shorter posts were natural.

We took pride in building the stage of well chosen timbers, and in making the parts fit snugly. The floor especially was laid as smooth and as evenly as possible; and here and there, if a crack appeared, a dry corn stalk was caulked in to make the floor snug and smooth. We were also careful to choose straight, well formed trunks for posts and floor beams.

Drying Rods

Lying across the top of the stage in harvest time, with their ends resting on the upper rails, were often a number of drying rods. A drying rod was a pole averaging a little more than two inches in diameter and about thirteen feet long, its length permitting six or seven inches to project over the rail on which either end rested.

These drying rods were much used in harvest time. When old women came to the stage to slice squashes, they spitted the slices, as I have described, on willow spits; and these spits again were laid on the drying rods, each end of a spit resting on one of the rods.

The drying rods had other uses. If the day was warm, old women working on the floor of the stage would lay two or three of these rods across the upper rails and throw a buffalo robe over them, and thus have shade while they worked. They bound the robe down with thongs to hold it firm.

When not in use the drying rods were laid lengthwise on the floor of the stage that the wind might not blow them about.

Other Uses of the Drying Stage

By far the chief use of the drying stage, was to dry our vegetables, especially our corn and sliced squashes. Firewood, collected from the Missouri river in the June rise, was often piled on and under the stage floor, to dry.

The keepers of the O'kipᶐ ceremony used to bring out their buffalo head masks, and air them on the drying stage that stood before their lodge door.

CHAPTER IX

TOOLS

Hoe

Iron hoes had come into general use when I was a girl, but there were two or three old women who used old fashioned bone hoes. I think my grandmother, Turtle, was the very last to use one of these bone hoes. I will describe the hoe she used, as I remember it.

The blade was made of the shoulder bone of a buffalo, with the edge trimmed and sharpened; and the ridge of bone, that is found on the shoulder blade of every animal, was cut off and the place smoothed.

The handle of the hoe was split, and grooves were cut in the split to receive the bone blade; this was slightly cut to fit and was so set that the edge pointed a little backwards.

Raw-hide thongs bound the split firmly about the blade and a stout thong, running from a groove a little way up the handle, braced the blade in place. (See figure 3, page 12).

Under my directions, Goodbird has made a hoe such as I saw my grandmother use, using the shoulder bone of a steer for a blade. You can make necessary measurements from it.

Hoe handles were made of cottonwood or some other light wood.

Rakes

We Hidatsas began our tilling season with the rake.

We used two kinds,[1] both of native make; one was made of a black-tailed deer horn (figure 5, page 14), the other was of wood (figure 4, page 14).

Of the two, we thought the horn rake the better, because it did not grow worms, as we said. Worms often appear in a garden and do much damage. It is a tradition with us that worms are afraid of horn; and we be-

---

[1] "The first that rakes are mentioned in the stories of my tribe so far as I know, is in the tale of 'The Grandson.' There is a little lake down near Short River where lived an old magic woman, whom we call Old-woman-who-never-dies. There is a level piece of ground near by, about five miles long by one and a half mile wide. This flat land was the garden of Old-woman-who-never-dies. Her servants were the deer that thronged the near-by timber. These deer worked her garden for her. All buck deer have horns; and with their horns the deer raked up the weeds and refuse of Old-woman-who-never-dies's garden.

"Now deer shed their horns. Old-woman-who-never-dies got these shed horns and bound them on sticks and so we got our first rakes. Her grandson saw what she did and afterwards taught the people to make rakes also.

"In later times we learned to make rakes of ash wood instead of horns; but we still reckon the teeth to mean the tines of a deer's antler. Sometimes deer have six, sometimes seven tines on an antler. So we make our ash rakes, some with six, some with seven teeth.

"If the Grandson had not seen what his grandmother did, we Hidatsas would never have known how to make rakes, either of horn or of ash wood."—WOLF CHIEF (told in 1910).

lieved if we used black-tailed deer horn rakes, not many worms would be found in our fields that season.

We believed wooden rakes caused worms in the corn. These worms, we thought, came out of the wood in the rakes; just how this was, we did not know.

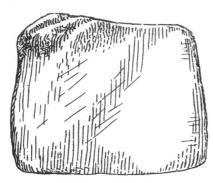

Figure 35

However, horn rakes were heavy and rather hard to make; and for this reason, the handier and more easily made wooden rakes were more commonly used.

All this that I tell you of our tools and fields is our own lore. White men taught us none of it. All that I have told you, we Indians knew since the world began.

Squash Knives

Squash knives of bone were still in use when I was young. I have often seen old women using them but, as I recollect, I never saw one being made.

The knife was made from the thin part of a buffalo's shoulder bone; never, I think, from the shoulder bone of a deer, elk, or bear.

The bone of a buffalo cow was best, because it was thinner. If the squash knife was too thick, the slices of squash were apt to break as they were being severed from the fruit. Bone squash knives, as I remember, were used for slicing squashes and for nothing else.

A squash knife should be cut from green bone; it would then keep an edge, for green bone is firm and hard. I do not think I ever saw anyone sharpening a bone knife so far as I can now recollect.

There was no handle to a bone squash knife, beyond the natural bone.

A bone squash knife lasted a long time. Old women in our village who used these bone knives, brought them out each summer in the squash harvest. It was their habit, I think, to keep the knives in the back part of the lodge, by the owner's bed. Whether it was customary to keep the knives in bags, or in some other receptacle, I do not know.

My mothers used a white man's steel knife for slicing squashes; but as I have said, there were old women in the village who still used the older bone knives.

Yellow Squash, I remember, was one; an old Hidatsa woman named Blossom was another; so also was Goes-around-the-end.

This model of a squash knife (figure 35) that I have had my son Goodbird make for you, is of rather dry bone; I have had him grease it, that it may be more like green bone.

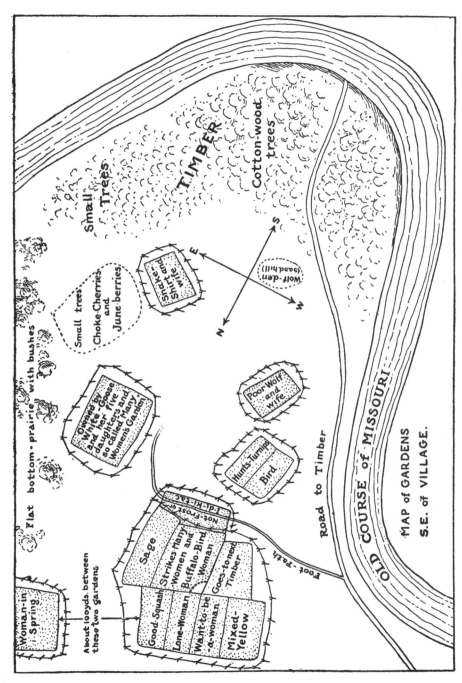

Figure 36

CHAPTER X

FIELDS AT LIKE-A-FISHHOOK VILLAGE

East-Side Fields

Figure 36 is a map I have made of the gardens east, or better, southeast, of Like-a-fishhook village. The fields lay, as indicated on the map, upon a point of land that went out into the Missouri river. The map is only approximately correct. There were many other gardens than those represented here on the map; for I have made no attempt to indicate any but those that lay in the immediate vicinity of the field my family tilled. These, however, I remember pretty clearly, and believe my map to be, as far as it goes, fairly accurate.

Our family garden is the one marked "Strikes-many-women's and Buffalobird-woman's." It lay just south of Lone Woman's and Want-to-be-a-woman's. The field was rather irregular at first; a corner of it, as I have said, was claimed by Lone Woman and Goes-to-next-timber, as they had started to clear it. My mothers bought out the rights of the claimants, in order to keep our field more nearly rectangular, so that we could count our Indian acres more accurately. This corner is marked by a dotted line, on the map.

I remember that when I was a little girl, the boundaries of the field were rather irregular at first; and my grandmother, Turtle, would go along the edge with her digging stick and dig up the ground to make the corners come out more nearly squared, and the sides of the field be straightened.

The field was also enlarged from year to year toward the sides; and much of this work my grandmother did with her digging stick. The garden when completed was the largest ever owned in my family; it was this field whose size I measured off for you on the prairie the other day.

The village gardens varied in size. Some families tilled large fields; others rather small ones. Some families did not work very energetically; and these were often put to it to have food. Other families worked hard, and always had a plenty. Families were not all equally industrious.

There were no watchers' stages nor booths in these east-side fields. The ground rose in a shelf, or bluff, just north of the gardens; from this shelf the watchers could watch their fields and sing to the growing corn without the trouble of having to build stages.

The soil of the east-side gardens was bottom land and prairie, with little or no timber.

East Side Fences

Our fields on the east-side of the village were fenced, as will be seen from the map. The fences were made thus:

Posts were cut of any kind of wood two or three inches in diameter and forked at the top. These were set in holes, at distances about as we now use for corral posts, or twelve feet from post to post. Posts were sunk the length of my forearm and fingers into the ground. Holes were made with digging stick and knife, and the dirt drawn out by hand.

Rails were laid in the forks of the posts and bound down with strips of bark; elm bark was strongest, but other kinds were used. The railing thus made ran about three and a half feet from the ground, the height of the posts that upheld it. All the rails were peeled of bark.

No attempt was made to firm the structure, as we did our drying stages. Our object was but to keep out the horses, and if the fence was strong enough to withstand the winds we thought that enough.

As will be seen from the map, some of the fields were fenced quite around; but this was done only when the field was isolated. When several gardens adjoined, a single fence usually ran around them all, and not around each individual field.

When several gardens were enclosed in a single fence, each owner looked after that part of the fence that bordered her own land, and kept it in repair.

We did not run our fences close to the boundary of our gardens as white men do. As we built our fences chiefly to keep horses out of the gardens, we placed them far enough away so that even if the horses approached the fence, they could not reach over and nibble the growing corn.

I think our fences stood twelve or fifteen feet away from the cultivated ground, as I pace it here on the ground. I know no reason why they were run thus, except as I have said, to keep the horses from nibbling the corn. You see, fifteen feet is quite a little distance; and the fence could have stood closer to the cultivated ground and still been far enough away to keep the horses from nibbling the crops. All I know is, that it was a custom of my tribe, and I always followed this custom if I had a fence to build.

As will be seen by the map, the corners of the fences were turned rather round; not built squared, as white men build their fences. We could not square the corners as white men do when they build wire fences, because we could not lay the rails in the forks of the posts and bind them down firmly if we did so. Perhaps that is the reason we ran the fences so far from the cultivated ground, that the fence, turning the corners, might not invade the cultivated ground—if you will look at the map you will see what I mean. However, I do not know if this is the reason or not.

Horses did not trouble us much, as we did not permit them to graze near our garden lands; they were pastured on the prairie.

We always had fences around our fields as long ago as I know any-thing about; and I have heard that our tribe had such fences in the villages they built at the mouth of the Knife River, to protect their fields there

from their horses.   Such, I have heard, has been our Indian custom since
the world began.

At the very first it is true, we did not own ponies; but we soon got them.

I think my tribe obtained ponies from the western tribes.   In my own
youth we Hidatsas got many of our horses from western tribes, especially
from the Crows.

Idikita'c's Garden

On the map there appears a garden marked as belonging to a woman
named Idikita'c.   She made her garden after all the others had been fenced
in.   There was a road that went down to some June-berry and choke-cherry
patches, in the small timber that stood beyond the gardens; it was a mere
path used by villagers afoot, by women with their dogs, and sometimes by
horsemen.

Now, Idikita'c laid out her field so that it enclosed a small section of
this road; and she built a fence around it and tried to keep the villagers
from going across her land.   The people did not like this.   Idikita'c would
tie up her fence tight, but the villagers going down to the choke-cherry
patch, would go right through her garden, following the road that had been
there; sometimes they even went through with horses.

"You must not make your garden here," the people said to Idikita'c,
"this is a road!"

And Idikita'c answered, "I do not want you to do damage to my garden!"

There was quite a deal of talk in the village about this matter, and
quite a bit of trouble came of it.

Fields West of the Village

The first field cleared by my father's family on the west side of the village, is that marked *A*, on the plot legended with Turtle's name, on the map
(figure 37), which I have had my son Goodbird draw for you of our west-
side fields.   A coulee bordered one end of the field; and in the rainy months
the water washed out much of the good soil.   Willows growing up along
the edge of the coulee also gave us much trouble.   We therefore extended
our field to the other side of the coulee, to include the part marked *B*.

Afterwards we added another field, marked on the map with my name,
Maxi'diwiac.

In Turtle's garden there was a watchers' stage, *C*, with a tree beside it.
There was also a booth, *D*.

Peppermint and Yellow Hair had each a watchers' stage and a booth
in her garden, as indicated on the map.   Another stage and a tree stood
in a garden near by, the name of whose owner I have now forgotten.   I
have marked the position of stage and tree in each field only approximately

except in Turtle's garden; as this was one of our own family fields, I remember the position of stage and tree very accurately.

In this map, as in that of the east-side gardens, I have indicated only the fields that lay in the vicinity of those cultivated by my own family;

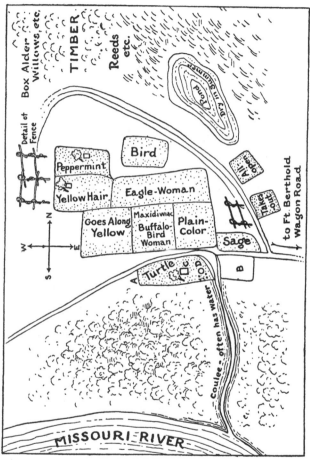

Figure 37

there were many others, but I can not, after so many years, accurately mark their positions, nor tell the names of the owners.

West-Side Fence

A fence protected our west-side gardens also, but only on the side nearest the village, probably because the horses could be expected to come from that direction. This fence differed somewhat from those on the east side.

The fence was built thus:

A heavy stick was sharpened at one end and driven into the ground with an ax; it was loosened by working it from side to side with the hands, and withdrawn, leaving a hole about a foot deep.

Into this hole was thrust a diamond willow, butt end downward, for post. The long tapering top with the twigs and leaves still on it, was bent over and around a rail (that was raised into position for the purpose) and then twisted around the post and tied down with bark. A second rail was bound to the post below the first. The sketch on the map gives an idea of what is meant, and in figure 38 is sketch and diagram by Goodbird.

Figure 38

Reproduced from sketch by Goodbird. On the left is post newly placed with foliage intact. On the right is post with foliage omitted to show how top was bound down over rails.

This fence was nearly or quite shoulder high to a woman, or about four feet; and the posts were about two feet apart, so that even a traveller going afoot could not squeeze his way between them.

Crops, Our First Wagon

The first wagon owned in my tribe belonged to Had-many-antelopes. My father hired him for a pair of trousers to haul in the corn from our gardens, one year. Had-many-antelopes fetched in three wagon loads from my garden; the field I mean, marked with my name; and three more wagon loads from the field *A*, in Turtle's garden. From the field *B*, in Turtle's garden, the family fetched the corn that year, for that field we had planted all to sweet corn; not gummy corn, but corn planted to half-boil and dry, for winter.

CHAPTER XI

MISCELLANEA

Divisions Between Gardens

When two fields adjoined the dividing space, or ground that ran between them, we called maądupatska'; it was always about four feet wide.

The word really means, I think, a raised ridge of earth. We still use the word in this sense. Down by the government school house at Independence, our agent has run a road; and the earth dug out of the roadway has been piled along the side in a low ridge to get rid of it. This ridge, running along the side of the road, we call maądupatska'.

But the maądupatska' dividing two gardens in old times was never raised in a ridge. It was nothing but a four-foot-wide dividing line. Nothing grew on it. Each gardener hoed her half of the maądupätska' to keep it clean of grass and weeds. We were particular about this; we did not want to have any weeds in our gardens.

I do not mean that I, for example, was accustomed to hoe exactly one half of the maądupatska' that bordered my garden, leaving exactly the other half to my neighbor. I merely hoed as needed, and my neighbor did likewise; but the work was pretty equally divided, each woman recognizing that she should do her share.

Sometimes, however, the owner of a garden would come to her next neighbor and say, "I do not want you to have any hard feelings, nor speak against me; but I want to plant the maądupatska' that divides our gardens, in squash;" or instead of squash, she might want to plant it in sunflowers or beans.

Permission being given, she would plant as she had requested; and thereafter, of course, she would hoe all the maądupatska', because she had a crop standing on it. But even then the ground would not be hers, and her neighbor might refuse the permission asked.

I have said that it might be asked to plant squash, or beans, or sunflowers. A gardener never asked to plant corn on the maądupatska' that bordered her field. Rows of corn hills should be about four feet apart; and as this was the width of the maądupatska', even a single row of hills would have crowded the corn; but beans or squashes or sunflowers planted on the maądupatska' did not do so.

Fallowing, Ownership of Gardens

The first crop on new ground was always the best, though the second was nearly as good. The third year's crop was not so good; and after that,

113

each year, the crop grew less, until in some seasons, especially in a dry summer, hardly anything was produced.

The owners then stopped cultivating the garden and let it lie for two years; the third year they again planted the garden and found it would yield a good crop as before. During the two years their garden lay fallow, the family owning it would plant their season's crop elsewhere.

In my father's family we owned garden lands both on the east and on the west side of the village, as I have told you in explaining the two maps made for you. This made it easy, if need arose, to work one garden while we let the other rest. There were families in the village who owned more fields even, than did my father's household.

Sometimes when a woman died, her relatives did not trouble themselves to work her garden for a couple of years, but just let it rest; then they would begin planting it again, and the ground was sure to bring forth a good crop. I think our custom of fallowing ground may have arisen in this way. When a woman died leaving a garden, and her relatives did not at once take possession, it was found that a two years' rest increased the yield; and so the custom of fallowing, perhaps, arose. Every one in the village knew the value of a two years' fallowing.

Ground that was newly broken produced good crops for a long time. Our family's west side garden once got to producing very poor crops; and we let it lie untilled for two years. I do not recollect how long it was before we let it rest again.

There was no rule how long we should use land before we fallowed it; nor was there any rule that we should let it rest for just two years. We merely knew that two years' rest brought a poorly producing field back into good condition.

Sometimes a woman died and her garden was abandoned by her relatives, who perhaps had more land than they could use. For this and other causes, there were always some of the cultivated lands of the village lying vacant. We never had all our fields in use every year; there were always some lying untilled, either for fallowing, or for some other reason.

If a woman died and her relatives did not care to till her garden, it was free to any one who cared to make use of it. However, if a woman desired to take possession of such an abandoned field, it was thought right that she should ask permission of the dead owner's relatives. Permission might be asked of the dead woman's son, or daughter, her mother, her husband's sister, or of the husband himself.

The woman did not wait two years before asking; if she wanted the dead woman's field, she just went to the relatives and asked for it.

When the owner of a field died, I never heard that her relatives ever sold it; if they did not care to use it themselves, they gave it to some one who did, or let it lie abandoned.

Frost in the Gardens

The fields that lay on the west side of our village got frosted more easily than those on the east side. Indeed, our west-side gardens suffered a good deal from frost.

The reason was that the ground along the Missouri was lower on the west side of the village; and fields that lay on lower ground, we knew, were more likely to get frosted than those on higher ground. Gardens on the higher grounds east of the village were seldom touched by frost.

Maxi'diwiac's Philosophy of Frost

Fields lying on lower ground catch frost more easily than those that lie higher. On a warm day, the ground becomes warmed; but at night cool air comes up out of the ground, and we can see that where it meets the warm air above, it creates a kind of snow [hoar frost].

Also, some days the wind is high; and toward evening it dies down. The hot airs are then sucked down into the ground and cause moisture to rise up out of the ground in steam. Afterwards, if the cool air comes up out of the ground and meets that hot air, it makes a kind of snow on the weeds and corn, killing them. But you can not see this steam until the cold air arises; then it becomes visible.

Men Helping in the Field

Did young men work in the fields? (laughing heartily.) Certainly not! The young men should be off hunting, or on a war party; and youths not yet young men should be out guarding the horses. Their duties were elsewhere, also they spent a great deal of time dressing up to be seen of the village maidens; they should not be working in the fields!

But old men, too old to go to war, went out into the fields and helped their wives. It was theirs to plant the corn while the women made the hills; and they also helped pull up weeds.[1]

When their sweethearts were working in the fields, young men often came out and talked to them, and maybe worked a little. However, it was not much real work that they did; they were but seeking a chance to talk, each with his sweetheart.

[1] "In my tribe in old times, some men helped their wives in their gardens. Others did not. Those who did not help their wives talked against those who did, saying, 'That man's wife makes him her servant!'

"And the others retorted, 'Look, that man puts all the hard work on his wife!'

"Men were not alike; some did not like to work in the garden at all, and cared for nothing but to go around visiting or to be off on a hunt.

"My father, Small Ankle, liked to garden and often helped his wives. He told me that that was the best way to do. 'Whatever you do,' he said, 'help your wife in all things!' He taught me to clean the garden, to help gather the corn, to hoe, and to rake.

"My father said that that man lived best and had plenty to eat who helped his wife. One who did not help his wife was likely to have scanty stores of food."—WOLF CHIEF (told in 1910).

Sucking the Sweet Juice

When the first green corn was plucked, we Indian women often broke off a piece of the stalk and sucked it for the sweet juice it contained. We did this merely for a little taste of sweets in the field; we never took the green stalks home to use as food at our meals.

Did old men do this, you ask? (laughing.) How could they, with their teeth all worn down? Old men could not chew such hard stuff!

No, just women and children did this—sucked the green corn stalks for the juice.

Corn as Fodder for Horses

In the early part of the harvest season, when we plucked green corn to boil, we gathered the ears first; afterwards we gathered the green stalks from which the ears had been stripped. These stalks with the leaves on them we fed to our horses, either without the lodge, or inside, in the corral.

We commonly husked our corn, as I have said, out in the fields, piling up the husks in a heap. After the corn was all in, we drove our horses to the field to eat both the standing fodder and the husks that lay heaped near the husking place. Horses readily ate corn fodder, and by the time spring came again, there was little left in the field; not only were the husks devoured, but most of the standing stalks were eaten off nearly or quite to the ground.

Disposition of Weeds

Weeds that we cut down in hoeing a field, we let lie on the ground if they were young weeds and bore no seeds nor blossoms, but if the weeds had seeded, we bore them off the garden about fifteen or twenty yards from the cultivated ground and left them to rot.

In olden times we Indian women let no weeds grow in our gardens. I was very particular about keeping my own garden clean all the time.

The Spring Clean-up

We never bothered to burn weeds; but in the spring we always cleaned up our fields before planting. We pulled up the stubs of corn stalks and roots, and piled them with the previous year's bean vines and sunflower stalks, in the middle of the garden and burned them; this was commonly done at the husking place, where the husks had been piled. There was not a great deal of refuse left from the corn crop, however, as the horses had eaten most of it for fodder in the previous fall; but bean vines they would not eat.

I never saw any one fire their corn stalks in the fall. Our yearly clean-up was always in the spring, when every field must be raked and cleaned before planting.

Manure

We Hidatsas did not like to have the dung of animals in our fields. The horses we turned into our gardens in the fall dropped dung; and where they did so, we found little worms and insects. We also noted that where dung fell, many kinds of weeds grew up the next year.

We did not like this, and we therefore carefully cleaned off the dried dung, picking it up by hand and throwing it ten feet or more beyond the edge of the garden plot. We did likewise with the droppings of white men's cattle, after they were brought to us.

The dung of horses and cattle raised sharp thistles, the kind that grows up in a big bush; and mustard, and another plant that has black seeds. These three kinds of weeds came to us with the white man; other weeds we had before, but they were native to our land.

Our corn and other vegetables can not grow on land that has many weeds. Now that white men have come and put manure on their fields, these strange weeds brought by them have become common. In old times we Hidatsas kept our gardens clean of weeds. I think this is harder to do now that we have so many more kinds of weeds.

I do not know that the worms in the manure did any harm to our gardens; but because we thought it bred worms and weeds, we did not like to have any dung on our garden lands; and we therefore removed it.

Worms

Our corn, we knew, raised a good many worms. They came out in the ears; it was the corn kernels that became the worms. Wood also became worms. Leaves became worms. All these bred worms of themselves.

I knew also, when I was a young woman, that flies lay eggs, that after a time the eggs move about alive; and that later these put on wings and fly away. Whether all flies do this, I did not know, but I knew that some do.

Many worms appeared in our gardens in some years; in other years they were fewer.

Wild Animals

Did buffaloes or deer ever raid our gardens? (laughing.) No. Buffaloes have keen scent, and they could wind an Indian a long way off. While they could smell us Indian people, or the smoke from our village, there was no danger that they would come near to eat our crops.

Antelopes lived out on the plains, in the open country; they never came near our fields.

Rocky Mountain sheep lived in the clay hills, in the very roughest country, where cedar trees and sage brush grow.

Black-tailed deer lived far away in the Bad Lands, in the little round patches of timber that are found there, where the country is very rough. They were not found near our village, nor in such places as those in which we planted our gardens.

White-tailed deer, however, lived in the heavy timber that lines the banks of the Missouri river. A few are still found on this reservation. However, though haunting the woods near our gardens, these deer never molested our crops; they never ate our corn ears nor nibbled the stalks.

About Old Tent Covers

I have said that we made the threshing booth under the drying stage, of an old tent cover.

Buffalo hides that we wanted to use for making tent covers, were taken in the spring when the buffaloes shed their hair and their skins are thin. The skin tent cover which we then made would be used all that summer; and the next winter, perhaps, we would begin to cut it up for moccasins. The following spring, again, we could take more buffalo hides and make another tent cover.

Not all families renewed a tent so often. Some families used a tent two years, and some even a much longer time; but many families used a tent cover but a single season. It was a very usual thing for the women of a family to make a new tent cover, in the spring.

Old tent covers, as I have said, were cut up for moccasins, or they were put to other uses. There was always a good deal of need about the lodge for skins that had been scraped bare of hair; and the skins in a tent cover were, of course, of this kind. Every bed in the earth lodge, in old times, was covered with an old tent cover.

Skins needed in threshing time were partly of these bed covers, taken down from the beds. Often the piece of an old tent cover from which we had been cutting moccasins would be brought out and used. Then we commonly had other buffalo hides, scraped bare of hair, stored in the lodge, ready for any use.

Buffaloes were plentiful in those days, and skins were easy to get. We had always abundance for use in threshing time.

CHAPTER XII

SINCE WHITE MEN CAME

How We Got Potatoes and Other Vegetables

The government has changed our old way of cultivating corn and our other vegetables, and has brought us seeds of many new vegetables and grains, and taught us their use. We Hidatsas and our friends, the Mandans, have also been removed from our village at Like-a-fishhook bend, and made to take our land in allotments; so that our old agriculture has in a measure fallen into disuse.

I was thirty-three years old when the government first plowed up fields for us; two big fields were broken, one between the village and the agency, and another on the farther side of the agency.

New kinds of seeds were issued to us, oats and wheat; and we were made to plant them in these newly plowed fields. Another field was plowed for us down in the bottom land along the Missouri; and here we were taught to plant potatoes. Each family was given a certain number of rows to plant and cultivate.

At first we Hidatsas did not like potatoes, because they smelled so strongly! Then we sometimes dug up our potatoes and took them into our earth lodges; and when cold weather came, the potatoes were frozen, and spoiled. For these reasons we did not take much interest in our potatoes, and often left them in the ground, not bothering to dig them.

Other seeds were issued to us, of watermelons, big squashes, onions, turnips, and other vegetables. Some of these we tried to eat, but did not like them very well; even the turnips and big squashes, we thought not so good as our own squashes and our wild prairie turnips. Moreover, we did not know how to dry these new vegetables for winter; so we often did not trouble even to harvest them.

The government was eager to teach the Indians to raise potatoes; and to get us women to cultivate them, paid as much as two dollars and a half a day for planting them in the plowed field. I remember I was paid that sum for planting them. After three or four years, finding the Indians did not have much taste for potatoes and rather seldom ate them, our agent made a big cache pit—a root cellar you say it was—and bought our potato crop of us. After this he would issue seed potatoes to us in the spring, and in the fall we would sell our crop to him. Thus, handling potatoes each year, we learned little by little to eat them.

The New Cultivation

The government also broke up big fields of prairie ground, and had us plant corn in them; but these fields on the prairie near the hills I do not think are so good as our old fields down in the timber lands along the Missouri. The prairie fields get dry easily and the soil is harder and more difficult to work.

Then I think our old way of raising corn is better than the new way taught us by white men. Last year, 1911, our agent held an agricultural fair on this reservation; and we Indians competed for prizes for the best corn. The corn which I sent to the fair took the first prize. I raised it on new ground; the ground had been plowed, but aside from that, I cultivated the corn exactly as in old times, with a hoe.

Iron Kettles

The first pots, or kettles, of metal that we Hidatsas got were of yellow tin [brass]; the French and the Crees also traded us kettles made of red tin [copper].

As long as we could get our native clay pots, we of my father's family did not use metal pots much, because the metal made the food taste. When I was a little girl, if any of us went to visit another family, and they gave us food cooked in an iron pot, we knew it at once because we could taste and smell the iron in the food.

I have said that we began cooking food in an iron kettle in my father's family when I was about eighteen years old; but the great iron kettle that lies in Goodbird's yard was given us by an Arikara woman before I was born.

CHAPTER XIII

TOBACCO

Observations by Maxi'diwiac

Tobacco was cultivated in my tribe only by old men. Our young men did not smoke much; a few did, but most of them used little tobacco, or almost none. They were taught that smoking would injure their lungs and make them short winded so that they would be poor runners. But when a man got to be about sixty years of age we thought it right for him to smoke as much as he liked. His war days and hunting days were over. Old men smoked quite a good deal.

Young men who used tobacco could run; but in a short time they became short of breath, and water, thick like syrup, came up into the mouth. A young man who smoked a great deal, if chased by enemies, could not run to escape from them, and so got killed. For this reason all the young men of my tribe were taught that they should not smoke.

Things have changed greatly since those good days; and now young and old, boys and men, all smoke. They seem to think that the new ways of the white man are right; but I do not. In olden days, we Hidatsas took good care of our bodies, as is not done now.

The Tobacco Garden

The old men of my tribe who smoked had each a tobacco garden planted not very far away from our corn fields, but never in the same plot with one. Two of these tobacco gardens were near the village, upon the top of some rising ground; they were owned by two old men, Bad Horn and Bear-looks-up. The earth lodges of these old men stood a little way out of the village, and their tobacco gardens were not far away. Bear-looks-up called my father "brother" and I often visited his lodge.

Tobacco gardens, as I remember them, were almost universal in my tribe when I was five or six years of age; they were still commonly planted when I was twelve years old; but white men had been bringing in their tobacco and selling it at the traders' stores for some years, and our tobacco gardens were becoming neglected.

As late as when I was sixteen, my father still kept his tobacco garden; but since that day individual gardens have not been kept in my tribe. Instead, just a little space in the vegetable garden is planted with seed if the owner wishes to raise tobacco.

The seed we use is the same that we planted in old times. A big insect that we call the "tobacco blower" used always to be found around our tobacco gardens; and this insect still appears about the little patches of tobacco that we plant.

The reason that tobacco gardens were planted apart from our vegetable fields in old times was, that the tobacco plants have a strong smell which affects the corn; if tobacco is planted near the corn, the growing corn stalks turn yellow and the corn is not so good. Tobacco plants were therefore kept out of our corn fields. We do not follow this custom now; and I do not think our new way is as good for the corn.

Planting

Tobacco seed was planted at the same time sunflower seed was planted.

The owner took a hoe and made soft every foot of the tobacco garden; and with a rake he made the loosened soil level and smooth.

He marked the ground with a stick into rows about eighteen inches apart. He opened a little package of seed, poured the seed into his left palm, and with his right sowed the seed very thickly in the row. He covered the newly sowed seed very lightly with soil which he raked with his hand.

When rain came, and warmth, the seeds sprouted. The seed having been planted thickly, the plants came up thickly, so that they had to be thinned out. The owner of the garden would weed out the weak plants, leaving only the stronger standing.

The earth about each plant was hilled up about it with a buffalo rib, into a little hill like a corn hill. It was a common thing to see an old man working in his tobacco garden with one of these ribs. Young men seldom worked in the tobacco gardens; not using tobacco very much, they cared little about it.

Arrow-head-earring's Tobacco Garden

An old man, I remember, named Arrow-head-earring, or Ma'iạ-pokcahec, had a patch of tobacco along the edge of a field on the east side of the village. He was a very old man. He used a big buffalo rib, sharpened on the edge, to work the soil and cultivate his tobacco. He caught the rib in his hands by both ends with the edge downward; and stooping over, he scraped the soil toward him, now and then raising the rib up and loosening the earth with the point at one end—poking up the soil, so to speak.

He wore no shirt as he worked; but he had a buffalo robe about his middle, on which he knelt as he worked.

Small Ankle's Cultivation

My father always attended to the planting of his tobacco garden. When the seed sprouted he thinned out the plants, weeded the ground and hilled up the tobacco plants later with his own hands.

Tobacco plants often came up wild from seed dropped by the cultivated plants. These wild plants seemed just as good as the cultivated
ones. There seemed little preference between them.

Harvesting the Blossoms

Tobacco plants began to blossom about the middle of June; and picking then began. Tobacco was gathered in two harvests. The first harvest
was of these blossoms, which we reckoned the best part of the plant for
smoking. Old men were fond of smoking them.

Blossoms were picked regularly every fourth day after the season set
in. If we neglected to pick them until the fifth day, the blossoms would
begin to seed.

This picking of the blossoms my father often did, but as he was old,
and the work was slow and took a long time, my sister and I used to help
him.

I well remember how my sister and I used to go out in late summer,
when the plants were in bloom, and gather the white blossoms. These I
would pluck from the plants, pinching them off with my thumb nail.
Picking blossoms was tedious work. The tobacco got into one's eyes and
made them smart just as white men's onions do to-day.

We picked, as I have said, every fourth day. Only the green part of the
blossom was kept. The white part I always threw away; it was of no value.

To receive the blossoms I took a small basket with me to the garden.
There were two kinds used; one was the bark basket that we wove, and
of which you have specimens; the other kind was made of a buffalo bull's
scrotum, with hair side out.

Such a basket as the latter was a little larger than the crown of a white
man's hat, the hat band being about the same diameter as the rim that we
put on the basket. It had the usual band to go over forehead or shoulders.
I bore the basket in the usual way on my back; or I could swing it around
on my breast when actually picking, thus making it easy to drop the blossoms into it.

More often, however, I took the basket off and set it on the ground
when plucking blossoms. I would make a little round place in the soft soil
with my hands and set the basket in it, so that it would stand upright. The
basket did not collapse, for the skin covering was tough and rigid, not soft.

I often used the scrotum basket also for picking choke-cherries or June
berries. It was more convenient when berrying to carry the basket swung
around on my breast. Going home with the basket filled with berries, I
bore it in the usual way on my back.

My father usually worked with us; and indeed it was to help him, because he was old, that we picked the blossoms at all. It was slow work.

I did not expect to gather more than a fourth of a small basketful every four days; and as the blossoms shrunk a good deal in drying, a day's picking looked rather scant.

When we fetched the blossoms home to the lodge, my father would spread a dry hide on the floor in front of his sacred objects of the Big Birds' ceremony; they were two skulls and a sacred pipe, wrapped in a bundle and lying on a kind of stand. We regarded these objects as a kind of shrine. Nobody ever walked between the fire and the shrine as that would have been a kind of disrespect to the gods. My father spread the new-plucked blossoms on the hide to dry. Lying here before the shrine, it was certain no one would forget and step on the blossoms.

It took quite a time to dry the blossoms. If the weather was damp and murky for several days, my father, on appearance of the sun again, would move the hide over to a place where the sun shining through the smoke hole, would fall on the blossoms. The smoke hole, being rather large, would let through quite a strong sunbeam, and the drying blossoms were kept directly in the beam.

When the blossoms had quite dried, my father fetched them over near the fireplace, and put them on a small skin, or on a plank. We commonly had planks, or boards, split from cottonwood trunks, lying in the lodge; they had many uses.

My father then took a piece of buffalo fat, thrust it on the end of a stick and roasted it slowly over the coals. This piece of hot fat he touched lightly here and there to the piled-up blossoms, so as to oil them slightly, but not too much. He next moved the skin or board down over the edge of the fire pit, tipping it slightly so that the heat from the fire would strike the blossoms. Here he left them a little while, but watching them all the time. Now and then he would gently stir the pile of blossoms with a little stick, so that the whole mass might be oiled equally.

This done my father took up the blossoms and put them into his tobacco bag. The tobacco bag that we used then was exactly like that used to-day, ornamented with quills or bead work; only in those days old men never bothered to ornament their tobacco bags, just having them plain.

When my father wanted to smoke these dried blossoms, he drew them from his tobacco bag and chopped them fine with a knife, a pipeful at a time. Cured in this way, tobacco blossoms were called aduatąkidu'cki. They were smoked by old men unmixed.

The blossoms were always dried within the lodge. If dried without, the sun and air took away their strength.

Harvesting the Plants

About harvest time, just before frost came, the rest of the plants were gathered—the stems and leaves, I mean, left after the harvesting of the blossoms. My father attended to this. He took no basket, but fetched the plants in his arms.

He dried the plants in the lodge near the place where the cache pit lay. For this he took sticks, about fifteen inches long, and thrust them over the beam between two of the exterior supporting posts, so that the sticks pointed a little upwards. On each of these sticks he hung two or three tobacco plants by thrusting the plants, root up, upon the stick, but without tying them.

When dry, these plants were taken down and put into a bag; or a package was made by folding over them a piece of old tent cover; and the package or bag was stored away in the cache pit.

When the tobacco plants were quite dry, the leaves readily fell off. Leaves that remained on the plants were smoked, of course; but it was the stems that furnished most of the smoking. They were treated like the blossoms, with buffalo fat, before putting into the tobacco pouch; we did not treat tobacco with buffalo fat except as needed for use, and to be put into the tobacco pouch, ready for smoking.

I do not remember that my father ever saved any of the blossoms to store away in the cache pit, as he did the stem, or plant tobacco. Friends and visitors were always coming and going; and when they came into the lodge my father would smoke with them, using the blossoms first, because they were his best tobacco. In this way, the blossoms were used up about as fast as they were gathered.

Before putting the tobacco away in the cache pit, my father was careful to put aside seed for the next year's planting. He gathered the black seeds into a small bundle about as big as my fingers bunched together, or about the size of a baby's fist, wrapping them up in a piece of soft skin which he tied with a string. He made two or three of these bundles and tied them to the top of his bed, or to a post near by, where there was no danger of their being disturbed.

We had no way of selecting tobacco seed. We just gathered any seed that was borne on the plants. Of course there were always good and bad seeds in every package; but as the owner of a tobacco garden always planted his seed very thickly, he was able to weed out all the weak plants as they came up, as I have already explained.

A tobacco plant, pulled up and hung up in the lodge, we called o'puti: opi, tobacco, and uti, base, foundation, substantial part.

The Mandans and Arikaras raised tobacco exactly as we did, in little gardens.

Selling to the Sioux

We used to sell a good deal of tobacco to the Sioux. They called it Pana'nitachani, or Ree's tobacco.

A bunch six or seven inches in diameter, bound together, we sold for one tanned hide.

Size of Tobacco Garden

My father's tobacco garden, when I was a little girl, was somewhat larger than this room; and that, as you measure it, is twenty-one by eighteen feet. I have seen other tobacco gardens planted by old men that measured somewhat larger; but this was about the average size.

Customs

If any one went into a tobacco garden and took tobacco without notifying the owner, we said that his hair would fall out; and if any one in the village began to lose his hair, and it kept coming out when he brushed it, we would laugh and say, "Hey, hey, you man! You have been stealing tobacco!"

What? You say you got this tobacco out of Wolf Chief's garden without asking? (laughing heartily.) Then be sure your hair will fall out when you comb it. Just watch, and see if it doesn't!

I have said that my father softened the soil of his tobacco garden with a hoe. After the plants began to grow, the hoe was not used, either for cutting the weeds or for hilling up the plants. I have said that the weak plants were culled out by hand, and that the strong plants were hilled up with a buffalo rib.

ACCESSORIES TO THE TOBACCO GARDEN

Fence

When I was a little girl every tobacco garden had a willow fence around it.

I remember very well seeing such fences built. Post holes were made by driving a sharp stake into the ground with an ax; the stake was withdrawn, and into the hole left by it, a diamond willow was thrust for a post; on this willow were left all the upper branches with the leaves. A rail was run from the post to its next neighbor, at the height of a woman's shoulder, and stayed in place by bending over the leafy top of the willow post, and drawing it around the rail, then twisting it down and around the body of the post in a spiral manner. If the leafy top of the post was long enough, and slender enough, it might, after being wrapped spirally about the post, be even drawn out and woven into the fence.

Below the top rail at a convenient distance, there ran a second rail, bound to the post with bark. Besides these rails, branches and twigs, and as I have said, the tops of the posts themselves, were interwoven into the fence to make it as dense as possible.

The posts of the fence stood about two and a half feet apart, making, with the rails and the interwoven twigs, a barrier so dense that even a dog could not push through it.

There was an opening left to enter the garden, closed by a kind of stile-bars of small poles thrust right and left between the posts; against these bars were leaned one or two bull berry bushes, which were removed when the owner wanted to enter.

If a weak place was found in the fence, it was strengthened with a bull berry bush thrust into the ground and leaned against the fence or woven into it.

The Scrotum Basket

I have said that we used a basket made of the scrotum of a buffalo bull, for picking tobacco blossoms.

A fresh scrotum was taken, and a rim or hoop of choke-cherry wood was bound around its mouth; choke-cherry limbs are flexible and easily bent. The hoop was sewed in place with sinew passing through the skin and around the hoop spirally.

A thong was bound at either end to opposite sides of the hoop, and the whole was hung upon the drying stage, or at the entrance to the earth lodge in the sun. The skin was then filled with sand until dry, when it was emptied, the thong removed, and a band, or leather handle, was bound on one side of the hoop, at places a few inches apart, and the basket was ready for use.

Figure 39

Reproduced from sketch by Goodbird.

The scrotum is the toughest part of the buffalo's hide. When dried it is as hard and rigid as wood.

Figure 39 is a sketch by Goodbird showing what the basket was like.

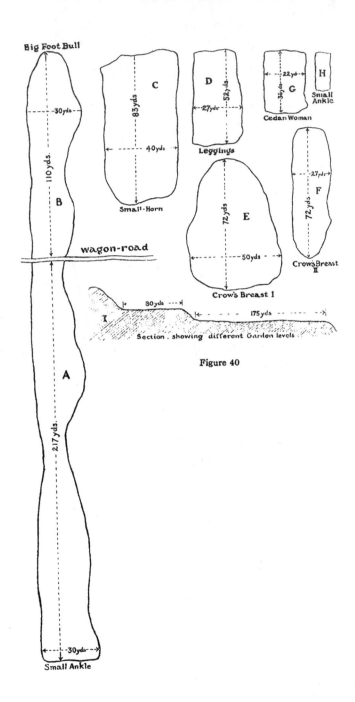

Figure 40

OLD GARDEN SITES NEAR INDEPENDENCE

Down in the bottoms along the Missouri near Independence school house are the gardens—now abandoned—used by the neighboring families when they first came to this part of the reservation, about 1886.

The fields are plainly marked in the underbrush and trees from the fact that they are relatively open. Goodbird accompanied me to the several locations and I made maps of the fields, which I include in figure 40. While not accurately surveyed—I had to pace off the distances—the fields are fairly accurately represented by the maps.

Figure 40, *I*, is a diagram in vertical section of the land surface in which the gardens lie. Toward the right is seen the basin of the Missouri river.

At the extreme left is a bit of the prairie that abuts the foothills. Between are two level terraces, one eighty yards, the other and lower, one hundred and seventy-five yards in width. Four of the gardens lie in the eighty-yard terrace; field *A*, of Small Ankle; *B* of Big Foot Bull; *E* of Crow's Breast, and *H*, a small bit of ground used by the Small Ankle family for a squash garden. Gardens *C* of Small Horn; *D* of Leggings; *F* of Crow's Breast; and *G* of Cedar Woman, lie in the lower and wider terrace.

With one exception the fields are called by the names of the male heads of the families, a custom that probably began at the time allotments were first made.

The relative positions of the fields are not as shown in the figure, except of *A* and *B*, the gardens of Small Ankle and Big Foot Bull. These are separated by a wagon road that descends to the lower terrace, as indicated on the map.

Doubtless the two terraces have been made by over-flow waters. It is likely that both are still subject to overflow at long intervals, especially the lower. The soil is light and sandy, but black and rich. The overflow of the river would seem to suggest that the land would be fertilized by silt deposited upon it; but my Indian informants seem to attach no significance to this. Fields were located near the Missouri "because the soil there is soft and easily worked, and does not become dry and burn up the crops."

GILBERT L. WILSON.